SUPERVISION AND COUNS

by
Gaie Houston

ACKNOWLEDGEMENTS

My grateful thanks to the many people I see and have seen for supervision, one by one and in groups, and to others, for all that I have learned from them about how to supervise.

My hope is that this book will help you to confidence, clarity, flexibility and rigour, and to pleasure in this aspect of your work.

CONTENTS

INTRODUCTION

Since this book was first published in 1990, a good deal has been written by other people on what was until then a remarkably undocumented subject. Some of what I wrote then does not, I think, need to be spelled out any more. As supervision is more recognised, ethical codes, and specific training, and the growing wisdom of the various professional bodies, supply part of what I felt I needed to write then.

In place of what I have taken out, I have made some additions. One of these is about direct supervision of groups. Then there is a philosophical piece, drawn from a talk I was invited to give to the Association of Humanistic Psychology, on the use and abuse of power in therapy. Another is a section on the Gods of supervision. There is more too about contracts with individuals and agencies.

As the title says, this book is designed both for supervisors and their supervisees, be they called counsellors, therapists or psychotherapists. At different moments supervision evokes the peer, parent, poet, and many other facets of both parties to the work.

From the moment we began learning to be counsellors, all of us were implicitly learning too to be supervisors to ourselves (Casement 1985). Supervising other people requires yet more vision and alertness, as we learn to scrutinise, to search to understand, sometimes forgive, sometimes celebrate, sometimes to evoke the illuminating image or change of frame in the supervisee. The work is evolutionary, in that it is often the shaping and informing of the next generation, in the hope that they can move far beyond where we have reached.

Carswell 1995

INTRODUCTION TO STYLE AND METHOD

You may prefer to start by reading the Practics chapter, about contracts and beginnings. But I was drawn first to this wider focus.

Three distinct areas of supervision include what I call *Policing*, which is to say all the boundary-monitoring which makes sure that there is emotionally and physically a clean and tidy place where both supervision and counselling can happen.

Then there is what can be called *Plumbing*, the how-to, teaching, competence area. The word is in memory of a psychologist I met long ago from behind the Iron Curtain, when that existed. He said in halting English that writers were the poets of the psyche. Psychologists were its plumbers. Plumbing may be prosaic, but is rather important. The plumbing in counselling includes having a proper knowledge of more than one theory of how people work; understanding something of the different mind-sets which occur at different times of life and in different cultures; being competent with some of the tools of the trade, some good-enough methods of working with clients. The counsellor's attitude, her patience and own mind-set are part of ordinary plumbing competence. A plumber who gets frustrated and kicks a leaky pipe may provoke a disastrous flood through a whole house.

The *Poetry* of supervision to me is in part all that subtle field described prosaically as The Working Alliance. It is too the creation of that free space where the supervisee lets herself tell back so that she hears herself afresh, and invent in imagination how she can best be for her client in their next session. It is where she can regain compassion for her client that may have been clouded by difficulties in their communication. It is where she, and the supervisor, are open to those intuitive leaps of insight and empathy which are not easily accounted for in rational explanation. Shelley said that *in the moment of inspiration, the mind is a fading coal*.

THE GODDESSES OF SUPERVISION

The myth of the Judgement of Paris involved three goddesses, who are another illuminator for these areas of supervision. *Hera* was the first, the wife of Zeus, and so the representative of power and authority, which takes in the policing function. *Athena*, the goddess of knowledge and wisdom, is a more graceful describer of what I have just called the plumbing part of the work. Last here, though first in the judgement, is *Aphrodite*, who stands for love, rapport, the emotional, the aesthetic, the interactive: in short, the poetic aspect.

At best, the way you supervise will be a unique mix of the functions these goddesses stand for: what you have learned, what you are skilled in by nature, and most formatively, your attitude. There is not one way to be a good supervisor. In your head you know that already. Please remember it again as you read what I say, or listen to other people's One Secret or Six Essentials of the subject. There are some drills it is as well to keep in mind. But much of this topic is outside the mechanically learned.

INTERVENTION CATEGORIES AND FOCI

One way to learn more about your style is to ask several of your supervisees if they mind you taping a session. Then you can listen back to yourself diagnostically. The process, the how of supervision, is of enormous importance. And so too is the content, the what-you-say. For this exercise, I suggest listening out, even scoring yourself as you listen for the categories of intervention you make. Many people find that they ask more questions than they supposed they did. This *Eliciting* style has its place. But questions are a form of control, in that they steer the other person heavily towards answering what you want to hear, rather than to what they might have been about to tell you. I like to ask supervisors in training to work for an afternoon without asking any questions at all, and without making question statements like "I am interested to hear more about..." After this, some decide that they only need ask questions when they need clarification of what has just been said. Others know that they work best when they elicit more than supply. *Eliciting* also covers giving free rein to the supervisee to supervise herself aloud in front of you, which is one of the most valuable services you can encourage.

CONTROLLING THE FOCUS

CLIENT AS FOREGROUND

Whether you make statements or ask questions, notice the focus of them. One is *Client-centred*, on the material of the counselling session, all that the client presented. The supervisor joins the supervisee in speculating about what may be going on for the client, in the hope that this enlarged field of awareness leads the supervisee to a larger strategy or range of responses. If you do a lot of this, you may need the reminder that you are getting a second-hand story from your supervisee. Some misrepresentation in this is extremely likely. Remember the old game, Chinese Whispers, in which messages are shown to become distorted as they are passed along.

Another aspect of client-centredness can be to discuss what the client did in the counselling session, with much less emphasis on the counsellor's co-creation of that session. When supervisees do this, I have often noticed that they are obliquely or directly telling me that they doubt if their part of that dialogue was adequate. So our conversation is likely to develop into looking at the client-counsellor system, and very likely to another shift of focus, to the counsellor herself. Before moving that way, I include a note on one method of making a diagnosis or formulation about a new client, which makes a frame for the supervisor's listening and response, as well as the counsellor's own work.

McHugh's *Perspectives of Psychiatry* (1986) are four foci which can help the counsellor to make a good enough formulation about a client. The third one, of observing actual behaviour, is being addressed by the counsellor who tells you and reminds herself of her client's mumbles or odd smiles or tendency to move a chair about or tread dirt into the room or whatever. Between the supervisor and herself, there can be clarity about whether she is moving herself towards more clarity about her intervention strategy, or is justifying her own seeming failure to reach this person.

When a new client is being presented in supervision, it is likely that more time will be spent talking directly about him or her, than later. The counsellor at this stage is searching to make enough sense of the wealth of data offered to her by the client, to settle on some strategy of how she is going to work with him. As a possible aid to organising this talk usefully, here are McHugh's four categories, in extremely brief outline. He recommends that you give attention to

1. What the patient is. This includes all that is readily measurable, like age, occupation, marital status, position in family and so forth.

2. What the patient has. By this he means the symptoms, disease or signs that you are told or otherwise become aware of.

3. What the patient does. This is the here and now of behaviour, and in time will include the habitual behaviours or others that are reported to you.

4. What the patient tells. This is the narrative self of the patient, as recounted to you. This is a rich area, the patient's understanding of his or her unique story. It is also one it is easy to dwell in overmuch with some people, to the neglect of the other areas of awareness.

McHugh suggests that it is never enough to pay attention only to some of these foci. Noticing all is being as aware as you can of the whole person. This applies as much to the way the supervisor perceives the supervisee, as the way the counsellor observes the client.

CONCENTRATING ON THE COUNSELLOR

With this focus, the supervisee tells back with as much detail as she can, or plays back from a tape, to put her own interventions under scrutiny. Notice, if this is your style, to what extent you let the supervisee account for what she did, and speculate on how she can develop the work. *Listening and Reflecting* may be the major interventions, if you do this.

Notice the frame in which you as supervisor do this listening. The benefit of the client is the main criterion by which you recognise or measure. A clever interpretation offered to this client may have academic status, but is of no use if the client finds it incomprehensible. A core-level

Rogerian reflection might sound a good response, in vacuo. But if it was made to a rather frantic inexperienced client who at that moment was demanding guidance, it may well have been received by her as stupid or hostile and evasive. Even if the counsellor for the moment is speaking of only part of the system of her and the client, the supervisor's work is likely to be to raise her awareness of the whole system, the context.

The temptation here and at many moments may be to be *Didactic*. There is a place for this, usually on a sliding scale, depending on the experience of the supervisee. Students in training may learn enormously from advice in this highly specific context. Even they probably have more repertoire of responses than you realise, if you butt in straightaway with suggestions. More experienced counsellors may be keen to sit back and have you solve their problems. If I notice that I have talked more than usual, and feel that I have said a few brilliantly insightful things, it is sometimes a sign to me that I have been hooked temporarily into a Please-Show-Me-Teacher game.

SUPERVISEE

SUPERVISOR

This *Information-giving* style is often frowned on. I have just described a place where I find it inappropriate. But most people have some gaps of understanding and knowledge. If they are little ones, and in territory familiar to the supervisor, I see a strong case for a bit of competence-raising by coaching or five minutes of tuition. The client is the person to bear in mind. Is he, is she, likely to be better served at this moment by you empathising with your supervisee's difficulties and tracing them to her own patterns of distress? Or would a few tips you know and that she obviously does not, about working with phobic clients or whatever, expedite relief for the client? Athena may supply the answer, at various levels.

SUPERVISOR AS CENTRE

Aphrodite is perhaps more in evidence in what can be called *Supervisor-Centred* work. This word is an attempt at avoiding the cumbersome phrase, Existential-Phenomenological. This focus involves attention to your own responses to what the supervisee tells and how she is in your session, and a careful telling back of your body-responses, and the images and thoughts that associate to them. From that base, you report or elicit surmises of how the supervision may be echoing the counselling itself, or echoing some scene in the client's life. The Echo chapter says more on this. This I-Thou (Buber 1970) style can be carried on one-sidedly. In supervision, the aim is for both people, or all in a group, to have a full part in the I-Thou dialogue. Thus the centre, or starting point, may be with the supervisor, but the field of discovery will at best be in the Aphrodite as well as the Athena domain. It is likely to be a direct expression of the profundity of people's perception and commentary (Houston 1995).

Just as concentration on the material of a counselling session will probably brings in much about the counsellor, and concentration on the counsellor probably brings in much about the client, so this *Supervisor-Centred* style at best brings in the whole field of the counselling: the client's world, the counsellor's world, and the supervisor.

For example, just reporting that you started to lose attention or wriggle your feet at a certain moment, may not enlighten your supervisee. That datum is a departure point, for noticing the connections of your behaviour, your response, into the field that is being created. You are both likely to discover more about what is going on between yourselves, and how that is a parallel process, an echo, of what is happening in the counselling.

THE TWO-WAY ECHO

Just as usefully, the supervisor here may be creating a new pattern, that will be taken back into the counselling. Commenting an irritation or confusion may be what is needed in the counselling.

I have come across people who talk about parallel process as one might talk about train-spotting: "I saw one!" They seem to assume that that is the end of the matter, and that the process will still roar away into the distance of its own volition, to be thought of no more.

Keeping an eye out for whether you are being an echo of the counselling, or are creating something that will re-echo there, is important. This idea is expanded in its own chapter.

STUCK-LIKE-IT

If you make supervision just like counselling, that is all it may become. The supervisee may drift into using her time primarily for her own soul-healing. This is a very important task. It is one proper to her own therapy, though. Good supervision will sometimes lead to a diagnosis of what needs healing, and to clarity about how clients can be protected from what has been stirred up in the counsellor. Therapy or counselling for the counsellor is the place for her to focus at length on herself. In supervision both parties are concerned primarily with her in just one setting, that with her client.

LIKE SUPERVISOR LIKE SUPERVISEE

The supervisor is an immensely influential person. You may have been more aware of that when you were a supervisee, than when you sit in the opposite chair.

Counsellors are very likely indeed to copy some of supervision when they are counselling. As supervisor you need both to be worth copying, and to keep an extremely lively eye on what is appropriate to supervision sessions, and less useful for the supervisee to take back as a method into her work.

The useful likenesses include among others

1. *Giving time to hear what is said and what needs to be said: deeply respecting the material.*

2. *Giving space to the client and to the supervisee to find their own answers.*

3. *Recognising and respecting mystery and not-knowing.*

4. *Maintaining confidentiality, non-discrimination and other boundaries .*

Some of the ways in which supervision may be different from counselling are

1. *Hera is present, in the codes of ethics and practice that both parties to supervision have agreed to. Both are liable to complaints being brought about their conduct.*

2. *Athena is present for both, in that an overview, and theoretical knowledge and skill are required from the supervisee, in a way they are not from a counselling client.*

3. *At times there may usefully be more I-It talk, reference to theory and method and ideas, in supervision, than in counselling.*

4. *At best the supervisor is free to be more unguarded in some respects than if she were working as a counsellor. Aphrodite may have a lively presence in shared confidences and problem-solving and more. This is a relationship between colleagues, which may for many people allow more informality than is proper in the counselling room.*

In time you will find the centre of your own style. You do not have to turn yourself into a copy or update version of someone else to be a good supervisor. Here, as in counselling, we have the magnificent opportunity to stay in what I call a working dialogue. By this, here, I mean a conversation in which there are clear rules and assumptions. A central one is to serve the client by doing whatever seems most likely to send the supervisee away more aware, informed, skilled and encouraged to be useful to her client than she was when she came in. For once in life, there is an overt contract for you to enable another person. It is hard for me to think of any more exciting, any more gratifying, task.

As in counselling, you know that this overall goal is not likely to be met by your offering metaphorical toffees. Short-term rewards may sometimes be bad for long-term health.

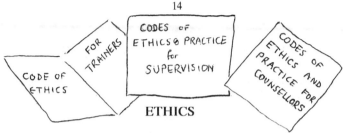

ETHICS

When this book was first published, far fewer counsellors were accredited than now. Now, most readers on seeing this chapter title will probably think of the printed codes of ethics and practice they are required to subscribe to by their accrediting body. Many of these codes stipulate that they must be read through with a new supervisor, so that both parties agree openly to work within their limits. There are also particular codes of practice for supervisors and supervisees, to take care of that relationship.

In this chapter are some aspects of these codes, and the informing spirit that needs to be in them, along with a little spillage into the counselling pair or group, and various practicalities which are the places where the ethics are both formed and demonstrated.

Whether she has noticed it or not, the counsellor or therapist always has her own internalised professional ethics. With the supervisor's help, she needs once in a while to talk these out. She is likely to be impressed and encouraged to work better when she reminds herself of her social goals, which is what ethics are about. Like all beliefs and rules, these are best left open to the possibility of change.

WHO IS IT FOR?

The first clarity which needs to be in place, which is there in all the supervisory codes of ethics I know, and is probably in the mind of anyone coming for supervision, is that the arrangement is primarily for the benefit of the counsellor's client, the invisible third party. This is the touchstone for many ethical and practical decisions in the course of sessions. In practice this means that the work of supervision sessions needs all to be directed to enhancing the therapeutic work of the counselling sessions.

People who come on courses for supervisors have sometimes said they are not always clear about the boundary between counselling and supervision. The criterion just spelt out here is the definer. The counsellor's distress or prejudice, say, is a topic for supervision insofar as it is impeding her work with a particular client, in definable ways. That distress or prejudice is a matter for her own therapy when it is in the foreground, pushing the client into the background for the counsellor. If this meant that a supervisee is not supposed to bounce into your consulting room and spend five minutes telling you she has just found she is having a baby, or has just been asked to sail the Atlantic, then life will be made drab by ethical considerations.

There is in fact relevance to clients in these life events, as there is in the counsellor's distress or mood. The judgement needed by both parties is to do with proportion. A counsellor who can keep quiet to what should be a trusted colleague about all new excitements in her life, may not create a climate of openness in her counselling room. And one who blatts on and on as supervisee, may well model excited reportage rather than reflective space, to the client. These are some of the many places where the supervisor's ethical stance as well as general wisdom need to guide her to comment or challenge.

WHO IS RESPONSIBLE?

Who is responsible for what? might be a clearer question here. There are many joint responsibilities, and some which belong with one or other of the parties to supervision.

Together, the supervisory pair need to have a contract or working agreement which properly embodies the codes of ethics and practice that both of them subscribe to, and allows too for what is asked for by any training or employing agency which is a party to their working together.

They both need to see what legal liabilities there are between them and with regard to the agency concerned, and most particularly towards the client. The Practics chapter says more which is relevant about this. As well as legal there are professional liabilities. So the supervisor needs to check that the supervisee makes her clients aware of any formal complaints procedure they may want to use against her. Complaints may be laid against a professional body and, or, within the organisation which employs or is training the supervisee. Everyone involved needs to carry suitable indemnity insurance.

It is up to both parties to say whether the supervision arrangement is working well enough, then to change how they work, or possibly, change the supervisor. This is part of the occasional review process that should be in the first agreement about supervision.

At least one well-known and respected code of ethics says that the supervisor is responsible for the observation of the supervisory and the counselling code of ethics. This can sound as if she is responsible for the supervisee's behaviour. This is a very large can to carry. It seems to me that the supervisor is certainly responsible for spelling out all she can that is likely to ensure that the client is properly placed and treated. This is her work and she needs to do it. But the supervisee is the person with the client; she is responsible for what she does there, and for reporting back adequately to the supervisor.

SUPERVISEE

This takes us neatly to the ethics and practice of being a supervisee. Real judgement is needed in choosing a supervisor. The most cosy person is not necessarily the one who will do best by your clients. Nor will you as supervisee do well by those clients if you are inappropriately selective in what you bring to supervision.

When you are in training, with very few clients, you will expect and be expected to talk about each in considerable detail. This helps you improve your diagnostic skills, and your skills of strategy, of clinical management, in the counselling. As you become more experienced, you need to be ever more selective about what you talk of in supervision.

Keeping your supervisor alongside about who you are seeing, who is starting and leaving, is a useful base of information. Then you will tend to talk about the people with whom you feel more at stretch or uncertain. And it is important from time to time to give some account of all the people you are seeing. Every so often there is a client who seems unproblematic, and so is not talked of much in supervision. Then one day you may decide you are going off track or feeling you have missed something, or are just getting bored - always a diagnostic clue, and one often better followed by two heads than one. The supervisor will likely be more help to you in such a case if she is told earlier rather than later.

Having some clarity about what you are seeing any client about, and what the general strategy is in your response, is a discipline more taught on some counselling courses than others. There is more about this in the chapter on record-keeping. It is another self-discipline which makes it easier to use your supervision time well: you have put in some tentative measures of how you are working with the client. Making a habit of talking through these diagnoses and strategies with your supervisor, when you begin work with a new client, probably increases the chances of your being more informed and more useful.

Hiding embarrassing errors from your supervisor is unethical and also a waste of the time and money you are spending with her in the client's interest. And I need to say that I am often impressed at the generous frankness of supervisees who report very fully on all kinds of lapses that occur, some of them more shaming than damaging, and some potentially grave.

Just as you and the supervisor both require you to be self-monitoring, it is up to you to keep an eye on your supervisor, and see that she is self-monitoring, and that she has not, for example, retreated into some ivory tower of seeming to know how things should be done, without getting out there and doing too much. Supervisors are not perfect people. I have come across one or two complaints about counsellors, which turned out to involve their having put enormous trust in the advice of supervisors. But the supervisors appear to have had dreadful judgement and little experience. It is not sneaky to keep an eye on your supervisor. It is a survival necessity.

SUPERVISOR

Near the top of the list is that fostering of an atmosphere of responsibility and trust that will let the supervisee feel as easy as may be in reporting her difficulties and mistakes as well as her competence. The chapter on rapport talks at greater length about this extremely important area, without which adherence to ethical codes and standards will be specially difficult for the supervisee, who risks becoming shamed or frightened or grumpy. And there is role-modelling in making a good job of achieving rapport. The counsellor needs to do something analagous with her client.

Another ethical issue which also has a strong modelling component, is in recognising the equal value and dignity of counsellors and their clients, whatever their race, status, sexual orientation, age and more that might be open to discrimination. This probably involves some specific training for the supervisor. It is easy to suppose oneself unprejudiced, until placed in a scene which triggers introjected attitudes. A gloss to all this is that the values spelled out by Carl Rogers, and embodied in much counselling training, whether Rogerian or no, are a positive expression of what is negatively termed anti-discrimination.

This leads to the ethical need for continued training for the supervisor, as part of the care for herself which will at best make her of more use to the supervisee and thus to the client. Training in supervision itself is becoming common, and will I imagine become mandatory before too many years have passed. As well, a good supervisor is in touch with life in general and with current developments in her field.

Films, theatre, books, television, are all also potential enlargers of the field of understanding and vision in which the supervisor listens and responds. Encouragement of the supervisee to continue her own education, even if she is already formally qualified, is an ethical requirement, too.

To keep your own work in perspective, as supervisor you need to have someone to consult. If, as is desirable, you work as a counsellor too, you may have a supervisor who is willing to allow some supervision monitoring and consultancy into the contract. This consultant or supervisor-of-supervisor is some insurance that you do not go on working when you are ill or depleted in some way that affects your judgement and your competence.

If you talk about your supervisee to another colleague, some part of the story of the client she sees are likely to travel to this next place. Confidentiality is another massively important part of all this work. In general I think it is easier for supervisors to keep confidentiality than it sometimes is for counsellors. The supervisor is already at a remove, or should be. Before taking on a supervisee, she needs to check, for example, who the supervisee sees for therapy. There may be a crossing of boundaries there that is best dealt with by sending the supervisee to someone else. Then, you will establish some agreement about using only the first name of clients, or no name, or a cipher.

Life gets more problematic when you realise that you know someone who is being discussed, even though their name has not been used. In the cases where this has happened to me, I have actually found it useful to have the extra knowledge about the client, so at times I have not divulged my near-certain guess, but have kept on working. If this makes you feel uncomfortable, then ask your supervisee to take that client to someone else; there is no need to go into explanations. If she has the tact to be in this work, she will not start prying.

Another sometimes awkward area is when a client is very secretive, and asks that the counsellor says nothing about her to anyone else. The counsellor is required by most ethical codes to have supervision, so this is not a fulfillable demand. Diplomacy often puts the client's mind at rest. Where it does not, there is an ethical issue for you and the supervisee to thrash out.

A similar issue is whether you advise your supervisee to tell all her clients that she will talk about them in supervision, and whether she tells them who the supervisor is. Recently a client sent a message to a supervision group I lead, that he did not want to be discussed there. One member of the group, his therapist, had told him she was in group supervision. In the event we had a conversation at abstract level, which established that when such a demand seems more to do with controlling the therapist than ensuring good practice, the counsellor must make her own decision. So in time this client was talked about, and the group gave what looked important encouragement to a counsellor who was beginning to be pushed around by a very distressed client.

More simply, as supervisor you need to be clear with your supervisee that you will only break confidentiality in special circumstances. One is for research purposes, or publication, with the supervisee's consent, and with proper disguise of the material presented. Another is where recommendations for professional purposes are involved. Alongside this is the need on occasion to break confidentiality in pursuit of disciplinary action, where the counsellor is in breach of an ethical standard. The client's good is usually the decider in such cases.

I add to all this what is called in law, the Duty of Care. This is a recognition that responsibility is not solely towards the person with whom one is dealing, but to comparitively powerless people who are closely affected by him or her. From time to time supervisees have used this view to bring themselves to confront a client, usually about maltreatment or potential maltreatment of a spouse or children. I see the importance of supporting such action, if necessary through to an appeal to Social Servicxes or another authority, if change does not happen. In the same way, as supervisor you may need to talk out with a supervisee what seems to be some unprofessional conduct, which may be detrimental to colleagues, say, or you or trainees or clients, or that in some way looks set to bring her or her profession into disrepute.

Every such case is painful, particular, and worth a good deal of thought and consultation before action. But gaffes have to be blown from time to time. It is up to you to say out, if you think your supervisee has a blind spot, or lacks specific training, or seems unreliable in one of a host of ways. The best will be that you can do this in a way that does not shame her into defensiveness, but brings out a new and useful development. It is when this one-to-one discussion produces no results that further action, preceded at best by careful explanation to the supervisee of what you see you will have to do, must be undertaken. The client is not well served if the supervisor is avoidant.

Another ethical question for the supervisor is about her distance from the supervisee. Making a friend or confidant of someone whom you first meet as a supervisee should not be undertaken lightly. And as in many matters, a useful guide is to think about how new to counselling the supervisee is. A trainee or fledgling probably needs to have strict boundaries modelled by you.

When you are a senior, the time may come when you know most professionals in your immediate field, and perhaps have peer supervision with one or with a group of them. By that time you should all be clear enough about the difference between what licence you will allow yourselves in supervision, and what is for much stricter observance in counselling. Supervision between peers can be very enhancing, if both people are clear that their affection for each other will not stand in the way of professional challenge and criticism where that is called for.

WORKING CONDITIONS

Besides the ethics which make the largest context of your work, I feel clear about insisting on the right answers to many, apparently small, particular questions. The supervisor needs to be sure, for example, that the supervisee is not working alone in a building, particularly at night.

I am thinking of one new drop-in counselling service that was set up just near a large psychiatric hospital in a large city. Until I objected, they took turns at having an evening alone in their Centre, which had the front door unlocked. Further, the counsellors in this new service all had perfectly respectable counselling qualifications; but none of them had experience of working with drop-out psychiatric patients dropping in upon them.

A janitor, a change to a by-appointment service, and their introduction to the nearby hospital, its staff and patients, were recommendations they accepted. If not, I would not have stayed as their supervisor. To my mind it is not ethical for the supervisor to gloss over the implications of such physical conditions, or of others, some of which are talked of in this chapter.

The working conditions round any supervisee who is attached to an agency need to be asked about and possibly spelled out in the contract you make as supervisor with that agency.

Anyone working privately needs to look after herself and her clients by having suitable premises and in some cases amenities such as an answerphone. In cities, an entryphone is next best to having someone to answer the door. The supervisor must check whether the counsellor lets herself be alone in the building with clients who pose some potential risk. Those in heavy transference, or of unstable personality, or under extreme stress, may not be best served by being alone in a premises with their counsellor.

Clear dealings about money are something the supervisor can model, and which she needs to monitor the supervisee with her clients. This is dealt with in Practics.

A rule of thumb is never to assume that your supervisee is being sensible in every respect. Check out. And stay with your beliefs. Do not go on supervising someone whose practices makes you uneasy. You choose whom to supervise. If that is not the case, change it. If you thoroughly dislike someone, there is perhaps little incentive for either of you to work together. If the other person seems mad, you may come to the same answer.

If you work in a training institution, supervisees may apparently be thrown at you in an arbitrary way. Elsewhere in this book I suggest the worse than uselessness of taking patients or clients just because they are Sent. Both parties to supervision, too, need to want to work together. If you quote the student who is so difficult that no other staff are prepared to take her on, then to me the large question is whether she should go on being a student at all. What is more, the open choice offered to her, to put some goodwill and effort into the supervision, or leave, can be a salutary confrontation. After they are in practice, I only want to supervise people I believe to be reliable counsellors. Moreover, just as people chatter about their therapist, so supervisees talk together about who they Go To For Supervision. Having them on my list or your list sounds like some kind of seal of approval of the way they work. Make sure you want to give it.

In supervision, I am there to be an effective supervisor, and to enjoy myself. There is more room for me in the group or partnership, at least in the way I supervise. I see this decision as an ethical one. I doubt if I could maintain reserves of patience for some difficult counselling clients, if I was constantly having to do the same with supervisees. I do not want to tell you to do what I do, but to notice that there is a choice there to make, and to be clear how you are making it and whether you respect what you decide.

At times I encourage counsellors to allow themselves a brief space to complain, whine, shout or in some way blow off some frustration. Likewise, I sometimes blurt, or say my scepticism, or devil's-advocate, or make faces.

You may prefer that whatever you say in supervision could be quoted to the counsellor's client without the slightest risk of offending her. That cautious position seems to me an admirable one, provided it suits your personality.

Usually I am remorseless in my assumption of everyone's personal responsibility. But circumstances alter cases. So I have an ethical requirement that anyone working as a counsellor under my supervision has at least a barefoot psychiatrist level of knowledge about signs of mental illness.

Counsellors are also likely to come across prospective clients who are on prescribed, or even illegal, drugs, or alcohol. There are ethical or pragmatic decisions to make here too. Again, they must be influenced by a counsellor's experience, or lack of it. As supervisor, you need to know enough to be able to discuss these difficult decisons in a way that is useful to your supervisee. Is she justified, for example, in saying that she will not work with anyone who arrives drunk or full of drugs? Is she right to say that she will not work with anyone who is abusing themselves with drugs or alcohol at all? Is it useful for her to counsel people on tranquillizers or mood-changing drugs? Is she going to insist on being in touch with their doctor if she takes them on? Does she look at these questions as ethical or pragmatic? How much are they either?

THE RESOURCE BOX

This is a file or box in which supervisees put copies of relevant

articles on these specialist subjects. As well, they amass there a list of publications, agencies and people who might be of help, including sympathetic local doctors and psychiatrists, mental hospitals, social services, day centres and much more. They may keep a simple drug list, one prepared by the local psychiatric hospital.

This is an age of information. Counsellors need easy ways of keeping up with what is happening and being thought in their area. I suggest that individual supervisees put together the same kind of file for themselves, and use the opportunity of training days or other meetings with peers, to exchange useful data. Doing such things is to me the demonstration of an ethical position, and a temperamental one. The counsellors are showing themselves still open to learning. One of the tasks of the supervisor is to encourage and maintain openness to learning from the outside world, and from the counsellor's own experience. The client will not get a proper service from anyone who has rigidified into an unquestioning orthodoxy in her work, or become a little vain about the correctness of her intuitions, or her general way of working. So, as supervisors, we need to work at staying as open and as sharp as we hope our supervisees will be.

PRACTICS

The first time you meet a new supervisee, a clear frame needs to be worked out with the agreement of both parties to it. The supervisee thinks out in some detail what she wants, and the supervisor does her best to keep in awareness the conditions of work that will leave them free to get on with the task, rather than keep re-defining boundary issues.

Practics is a word coined long ago by Katherine Whitehorn in The Observer. I use it here because it balances with the word Ethics, which heads the last chapter. The two interlink constantly. They are partly separated in this book so that the chapters will not be too long.

THE SUPERVISORY CONTRACT

The contract-making with which you begin any supervisory relationship needs to start with much of what is covered in the Ethics chapter. Here are more reminders of what needs to be agreed.

Different accrediting bodies have their own requirements for how many sessions of supervision counsellors have, in relation to the number of clients or groups they see. This I take as a minimum standard. Rather than just buy into it, I encourage prospective supervisees to consider whether they can in fact do with more. However many sessions they are interested in having, I see it as my job as supervisor to discuss with them whether seeing just me is the best. If some of their clients are a bit outside my experience, or at the edges of it, then I need to make that very clear, and maybe agree that another supervisor will deal with them.

Conversely, if a specialist counsellor who is supervised within her specialty, asks me to supervise a handful of other clients she also sees, I probably need to do some finding out before I agree. On occasion, people who do excellent work with, say, schizophrenic patients, or adolescents in care, or in an infertility clinic, turn out to be notably less skilled with the varied population other counsellors take in their stride. And these generic counsellors might be fairly flummoxed by the special needs groups such as those I have cited as examples. In either of these cases, provision needs to be there in your first supervisory agreement about renegotiating as you go along.

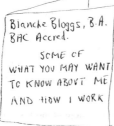

Blanche Bloggs, B.A.
BAC Accred.

SOME OF
WHAT YOU MAY WANT
TO KNOW ABOUT ME
AND HOW I WORK

Some supervisors like the clarity of a written agreement with every supervisee. It can be very helpful at least to have your fees and anything you want to insist on or talk over, on a written handout which can be sent to a prospective supervisee before you meet.

When someone comes to me off her own bat, rather than from an agency of any kind, I have so far always found a spoken agreement to work well. The definition of a healthy family, as one in which the rules are open, agreed, and subject to re-negotiation at any time, seems to me the best model for this understanding. So, in the case I have just suggested, we might set off with a talk about whether we seem to make a good pair, in terms of the strengths and the gaps in both our experience and trainings.

Then we may use the rest of the first session doing a piece of supervision, as a practical way of demonstrating our approaches, needs and methods.

When people come to you for supervision, as part of a training, there can be a particular conflict about the sessions. It looks as if many people are like me, in hating to do what I have been ordered to do, even if it is demonstrably for my own good. This is the major weakness of all statutory education. It breeds resistance simply by being obligatory. The following device has seemed specially useful to me with such people.

TIME TO DECIDE

Before the end of the first session I have with new supervisees or indeed counselling clients, I say that I would like them to go away and let a couple of nights pass, before telephoning me to say whether they would like to go on working with me. Commonly, they say that this is unnecessary, that they have made their minds up, that they want to get some dates fixed before their diary fills up, and so on. I stay with what I have said. The effect of this seems to be that the client is absolutely clear in her own mind that she has chosen to work with me. For people whose style is blame or confusion, this is important.

Generally, I know by the end of the first session with anyone, whether or not I am prepared to work with them. So I communicate this. They may argue that if I can know by the end of the session, then why can't I accept that they know too? Then I pull rank. I tell them that I have been working in this sort of setting for years and years. They have not.

On occasion I know when we meet that I do not want to work with someone. Perhaps they turn out to be in some category of people I doubt I can be useful to. Whatever the reason, I need to say if I do not want to go on. This only happens rarely, because almost everyone telephones before a first visit, and the chances are that I can learn enough, as you can, in such a phone call, to let me decide.

From time to time I can feel the need of the cooling-out period myself. I feel dubious but unclear. I probably want to talk in my supervision about the person now sitting in front of me. In that case, I say that the cooling-off time is for both of us to make up our minds whether we want to work together.

At our second meeting we work out the practicalities of time, place and frequency of meeting. Payment has usually been asked about at first contact; your fees and any special demands of yours, need to be in the other person's awareness before she says yes or no to seeing you, in any case. You may only be able to see her in the evening, or never then. Your work commitments or hers may demand some flexibility about when you meet in any week. There is a world of difference between having clarity about shifting times, before you begin, and on the other hand embarrassedly or apologetically or humpily playing it week by week.

You may require her to pay ahead, or at the time, or may bill her monthly and ask for payment within a certain time. You will have your own rule about whether she pays for cancelled sessions. She must have notice if you want to raise your fees. This is the sort of detail that can well be written down on a handout, to save time in the session, and the tedium for you of repeating, or forgetting to repeat, these infrastructure details

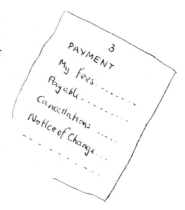

which may prevent good work if not attended to.

Doing what you can to make choice open to people is massively important in supervision and counselling. You may now be saying that this chewing-over time is a luxury not available for you to offer to prospective clients. Make it available. I say this with some force, from the conviction that you are undermining your own effectiveness if you work with people who have not decided for themselves to come and see you. You need to guard against the woolly thinking of people who say that if one alternative before them is unpalatable, then they have no choice. This is a very common way of holding on to bad feeling, of grudge about the choice that is made.

THE INFORMATION SHEET

It is worth pausing to recall one or two other of the topics that could be covered on an information sheet you put together. Details of your training and experience need to be set out. Your affiliations are important too. That gives a basis for talking through whether the codes of ethics and practice your prospective supervisee observes, are enough in line with yours for you to be in the same ball-park.

A politically hot question for you is whether you require her to subscribe to a code of ethics and belong to some professional body you have reason to trust. Supervision after all exists for the good of the client. Is it in the client's interests to have a counsellor who is not accountable, or about whom a complaint cannot be made except perhaps to a newspaper? And on the other hand, are you to cast someone out and refuse them supervision, perhaps in a region where there are hardly any suitable people for the job, simply because she never got around to joining something? You need to know where you stand, so that you do not waste the other person's time while you think all this out on the spot. And I hope you will let in some flexibility, so that you know where you stand, but feel able to move a little, without losing your balance completely.

If you like supervisees to bring notes or tapes to sessions, or invite you to watch some of their group time, or whatever, this needs to be spelled out too.

As you recall the things you say to every supervisee when you begin, or even the things you hope you have remembered to say, you will see more of what might constitute your idiosyncratic list of what can be written down on a handout, for discussion and negotiation after the supervisee has read it.

On this same sheet or on a form you devise, you may want her to write a note of her training, professional and supervision experience, memberships, personal therapy, work setting and extent, insurance and record-keeping.

> **5**
>
> ABOUT YOU
>
> Training - - - - -
> Qualifications - - -
> Accreditation - - - -
> Insurance Co and Number
> Last Supervisor - - - -
> Dates - - - - - - -
> Therapist - - - - -
> From - -

Confidentiality

Your proposals about confidentiality may be included, as both a statement about what you will do, and your wish about what she will do.

Asking your supervisee the name of her therapist when you start out, if she has one, is a good way of making a preliminary check about some possible professional overlaps. Being clear about confidentiality, and the times when it needs to be sacrificed, and how that is to be done, is a general area that needs proper attention. Most counsellors seem at ease with keeping totally quiet about their clients' identities, and, outside supervision, about them. Many are worried about violating confidence for the sake of the greater good, but are prepared to do so after proper discussion in supervision, in those very rare cases where it seems the proper course. In my experience this is not the problem. The most awkward area can be where professional lines are discovered to have been crossed.

PAYMENT

Not all, but a great many people who choose counselling as part or all of their work, seem comparatively uninterested in money. Certainly, if they were, they would be silly to take up a profession which is unlikely to make them anything in the way of a fortune. Since supervisors are likely to be of the same attitude, I think it is important not to collude in supervision at sliding uneasily round the taboos of fees and non-payments, and money generally.

There are exceptions. Peer supervision is payment in kind, and in my experience is generously feed in this way. Then again, giving supervision can sometimes be a way of helping a new voluntary agency or some other body to which the supervisor would like to contribute. There is something to be said for making a time-bounded contract for such an arrangement. It can be that the agency will begin to take a free service for granted, when it could be seen to be out of special need.

THREE-SIDED CONTRACTS

There are many bodies who employ counsellors, but whose managers do not understand too much about counselling. They are told that supervision is required; They fight for and succeed in extracting some funding for this activity, and after that feel hopeful that the whole question is off their probably crowded plate. As long as all goes easily, no-one may notice the gaps of understanding between the outsider, the supervisor, the counsellor, and her line manager, or whoever she is answerable to within the organisation, for her dealings with the people she counsels. The organisation itself, in terms of its policies towards employees, is almost a fourth party to the supervision arrangement.

CONTRACTS WITH AGENCIES

The Codes of Practice of BAC and other accrediting bodies point out that there needs to be a contract between the supervisor and the agency. In my experience, the agencies have much less concern about this. Busy people who in addition do not understand much about counselling often seem prepared or eager to throw some money in the direction of an outside supervisor, and see that as the end of the matter.

There can then be a perception from the organisation that the supervisor is responsible for the quality of the counselling offered. This increasingly is the sometimes covert expectation from within the profession itself, and I will come to my own views on that in a moment.

Looking first at what seems reasonable to negotiate between supervisor and funding agency, I see four areas to be worked through.

One is an acknowledgement of what the agency is offering me, in terms of money, time with their employees, space in which to meet them and their arrangements for termination or renewal of our contract.

Next, what I am offering can be explained, in terms of my qualifications and membership of a professional body, with its own complaints procedure which they are empowered to use against me if need be.

Then comes an exploration of what the agency is wanting from me. This conversation may turn out to be a piece of covert or open education of the relevant manager about the nature of the task. To me this is for the most part an examination of the clinical work of the counsellor or counsellors I shall work with, with emphasis on problematic material or problematic clients. At best I would like this to include identifying with the counsellor any professional development she needs and having a channel to communicate that to her manager, with a view to having that funded under any general staff development plan.

What I want from the agency includes some clarity about how and what and when we communicate. I favour a no-news-is-good-news approach, spelling out that if the line manager does not hear from me, she can assume that there are no insurmountable difficulties. But I want clarity that if I have serious doubts about a counsellor's work, and seem not to be able to resolve this after strenuous effort with the counsellor, I can involve the line manager.

I need too the recognition that I see it as part of my work to support the counsellors should they be complained against, but that this support has to be in ratio to the knowledge I have of them, and of the actions that are being complained against.

All this takes me to the murky and largely unexplored territory of supervisors and litigation. Most supervisors I meet are unclear about where their responsibility is seen to end. And there are not enough legal precedents in this country to give lawyers much guidance in advising in this area, either. The view I take, and which you have just seen I take care to embody in contracts where I can, is that I am not responsible for the actions of my supervisees. They act either in their own right, or as part of an employing body which has ultimately to carry the can. The supervisor is a consultant. Part of the counsellor's job is to find a competent consultant, and have enough judgement to **choose** well enough, and then to **use** well enough. The most competent supervisor cannot attempt to influence a piece of work she is never told about, or is lied to about.

But I do not see responsibility for eliciting the difficult areas of work solely with the supervisee. Part of the supervisor's work is to create the climate of confidence, and the judgement and self-examination that brings such material into the supervisory conversation.

On the other side, the supervisor's work is to use her best judgement at all times in the supervision. If it looks as if she colluded with bad practice, or advised it, so help us, that is a professional failure and needs to be dealt with as such, within the profession. In an increasingly litigious society, this may well mean that such bad practice will from time to time come to the law courts too.

There are very few precedents in this country about counselling confidentiality and the law. In theory disclosure can be demanded, and documents can be seized. In practice I know of cases where a supervisor has sat with a counsellor in court, and advised her or him on whether it would be in the client's interest to answer each question put.

The British Psychological Society takes the view that when a client quotes material from a session in order to discredit a counsellor, she is at liberty to say more about that session, in her own defence.

While hoping that you or your supervisees do not do anything to have yourselves complained about, these paragraphs are an implicit reminder to keep the law, like an angel of death, always sitting on your shoulder as you supervise.

MORE PRACTICALITIES ABOUT SESSIONS

What I do is what I am. How I supervise constitutes an ideological statement, whether I want it to or not. How you begin and end sessions is one of the many ways that what you do as supervisor may well be copied by your supervisee, when she is being counsellor. Notice what you are doing, and talk over with your supervisee any change you decide to make.

As I would when counselling, I like to deal with paying and any arrangements about the time of our next appointment, at the beginning of the session. That makes it easier to keep to time at the end. There needs to be some space between your sessions This timing reduces the likelihood of people meeting each other on the steps or in the hall, as well as giving the supervisor time for reading or briefly making notes, or just dashing about a little as a change from sitting still for a long time. A repeated drill of this kind is a reminder to the supervisee of the advantages of good time-keeping, of not arriving at the end of a perhaps emotional counselling session and then having to remind the client to pay.

I remember one supervisee who allowed a lot of time between appointments, in case her clients went on talking. Finally she understood that, without noticing it, she was setting up tensions with other colleagues. She discovered that local clients were beginning to say that if Mary let them have a nice long hour and twenty minutes or so, then why couldn't Betsy and Tim and all the rest be as sweet and understanding and accommodating? In other words, Mary had without noticing drifted into what she came to see as unfair competition with her peers.

It is easy to be aware of the limited system, the small context, of you-and-the-supervisee, or you-and-the-client. We are also operating in the context of our relation to colleagues, to institutions and work places and family. Indulging the Ancient Mariner in your client has effects not just on you, but through all those systems too, in a number of ways.

I have no mission to convert people to being perfect time-keepers. But I do know that unless I keep with fair strictness to my times when I am working, I am going to get frazzled, and encroach on the time of the next client. Time and again, I have a shrewd guess that I would also, in going along with the other person's hazy time boundaries, be ineffective. Consciously or unconsciously, they may use time as a weapon. I see it as my job to handle that weapon, show it to them, and maybe see if they are interested in turning it from a sword to a ploughshare, from a weapon to something useful. Just being bopped by the weapon, just being caught waiting for them to find their cheque book and diary, or tell me a last episode of their life story at the door, will not do that job for them.

SYSTEM INTERVENTION

Working out suitable interventions into a system is one area where supervision moves nearer consultation, with some benefit. Supervisees who are good at working in the small system of a pair or a therapy group, may not be much at ease in strategic thinking. Once more, as supervisor you are doing well if you let yourself notice and bring to the supervisee's attention this wider context.

As well as being explicit within a session, counsellors need to make themselves, and some hint of their way of working, known throughout any institution to which they are attached. At best, school counsellors occasionally take classes, and college counsellors take short courses, in which the values of counselling are demonstrated rather than just explained.

As supervisor you need to make sure that this part of the work is being carried out by any of your supervisees who work in institutions. Otherwise, at worst, the counselling service may become a strange ivory tower or even a white elephant within an organisation.

CURIOUS BEAST

RAPPORT, AND BEING YOURSELF

Interest, respect, honesty and warmth were some of the words that came up most often when I did a survey of supervisees' requirements of a good supervisor. So here is a chapter which I hope may remind you of some aspects of this foundation part of supervision.

What is the point of spending time, and probably money, going to see a supervisor with whom you feel so scared that you feel bad, or start to omit or invent or just lose interest? Daft. It is worse than that. Whether or not you mean it, you are likely to transplant into your counselling some of the attitudes you pick up in supervision.

As supervisor, you need to be open enough to yourself to know what you are teaching by example. I remember one of my supervisors, in many ways a very wise man, but reticent with his bad feelings. I can be better at that game than is good for me or honesty, so we sat there week after week inventing a world of reasonableness. He moved abroad, so I did not even challenge him about the tepid warmth between us, which had cooled to a setting point of boredom by the time he left. Then I went to someone who was a terrible intellectual show-off, and also talked into and over every sentence I started. She had so much to teach me that I put up with her style, while noticing how competitive and polysyllabic I became with her. We both smiled very brightly and nodded as we carved each other up verbally.

I learned something from these two, which I am reminded of time and again when I do live supervision of student psychotherapists. Dancing to the tune of the dominant member of a pair is a prevalent human response. A cheery counsellor may conjure false cheerfulness from a distressed client. A furious client may produce grovelling from the counsellor. The supervisor needs time and again to help the counsellor see herself as the patient probably does. Then they can work out whether the counsellor is pandering to the client, or fighting, or being in rapport.

Rapport is perhaps easier to recognise than to measure. As I think about it, I guess tentatively, that some of the people I supervise, those whose work I specially admire, seem to function on two levels of it.

IMMEDIATE RAPPORT

This is phenomenological, a response of the moment. It exists partly as physical feelings. In me they seem like a slight excitement in the chest. This I connect to a sense of a loss of fear of the person opposite, a confidence that we can, at least for part of our time together, be in tune with each other. The image that comes to me is of talking across a garden gate in good weather, rather than shouting greetings from our respective house windows. We are both within our boundaries, and yet we are close enough sometimes to touch each other.

My guess is that we are experiencing a form of synergy, an adjusting of my breathing and other body rhythms, even my brain waves, to complement, to be nearer the experience, of the other person. This rapport makes for an open learning and creative state. It has a lot to do with liking.

Each person shows herself, rather than edits herself first. When I have heard what I have said, I may disagree with myself. The other person's statement may sound nearer the truth - or further off. When we disagree, neither of us has the sense of attacking the other person or being attacked. We are searching to express something the best way we can.

This level of rapport is spun in the moment, and is vulnerable often to what the other person does.. Her change of expression, or brusque movement, or what she says, may influence me to be on guard, and so out of rapport. Out of rapport, I need to defend myself against her.

I want to maintain who I am and what I believe. I may start to feel hostile, as fear mounts that she is in some magical way threatening all that I am. As I have said, it is a dysfunctional state to be in constantly in counselling or supervision.

THIRD EYE RAPPORT

I said I suspect that rapport works at two levels. Perhaps a better description is of a spectrum. At one end is the truth of the moment, in all its simplicity and complexity of smell, sight, sound, memory, anticipation, the impact or lack of it of one person on another. This lively, fragile, moment-to-moment rapport is the stuff of intimacy and life, as well as some of counselling.

At the other pole is the ability to look at the person opposite in a large context, using a wide angle lens with great depth of field. The counsellor or supervisor, in some ways like a wise parent, needs to store up a data bank of rapport material. This has a lot to do with love, and with an awareness of more than the immediate present.

For psychotherapists whose method is to suppress many of their own immediate responses, in the interests of the transference, this level of rapport is important to their own psychic health as well as their patient's. Let me explain myself.

Your six-year-old is rude to a visitor, or kicks your shins, or in some other way hurts or shocks you. Unless you are very insensitive or over-controlled, you are likely to roar at her or hit back. In my view, and I hope in yours, only a scared and foolish parent immediately concludes from one piece of naughtiness that she or he is dealing with a child who is innately an evil being who from now on for ever must be controlled rather than trusted. Winnicott's good-enough parent recognises that the young kicker or show-off of this moment is the same child who gave her sweets to her crying sister, who, unasked, carried food upstairs to you when you were ill, who showed love and generosity in a thousand ways many thousand times in her short life. You still trust and love the child, the moment you have finished the frowning or yelling of the instant.

Counsellors and psychotherapists have a whole range of possible responses to a symbolic shin-kicking from a patient. Whatever they say or withhold at that moment, they need also to be aware of whether they have enough interest and belief in the kicker, to be prepared to go on working honestly.

When someone new to me in supervision begins to talk about a client as borderline, or possibly not ready for counselling, I wonder aloud about the counsellor's side of that comment. Yes, there are certainly people who can be described in these ways. But is this counsellor recognising something else which is valid and important to recognise, that her skills do not stretch to working with this client? Or is she saying that she simply feels frightened and vindictive, and has failed to recognise the stuff on which her underlying rapport databank could be built?

For example, however silent and apparently sulky a client is, she did actually get herself on the train and along the street and up the steps into your room. That is a statement of need or hope, of potential rapport, which is so obvious that in my experience counsellors often forget even to notice it.

Again, every rejection, distraction, over-projection, misunderstanding, dismissive response, piece of blame, of placating insincerity, half-truth, whopping lie, can paradoxically be used as material for your store of underlying rapport. The context in which I say this is my belief that people are intensely social creatures. We all want rapport, synergy, love, as a large part of our psychological, and so of our actual, survival strategy on this earth. If like me you believe this, then all the frustrating games a client plays are her personal failures, failures which by the time she gets to seek your professional skills, are probably deeply entrenched habits.

At another level, they are evidence of the amount of power, the amount of threat, she attributes to you, the counsellor. So I hope to look with some love at all those aspects of a client which in supervision may also make me groan and grimace about her. She is repeatedly showing me, for example, how she keeps herself lonely or disliked.

Looking with what in some belief systems is called the third eye, I may know the uselessness of re-enacting The Other, who usually walks out or shouts back or sneers or does whatever the client seems literally hell-bent on cajoling me to do. I feel in my bones, as you probably do, that if I start off a session feeling defensive, grim, narrow-eyed, I have probably reduced to zilch my chances of doing any useful work for the client or the supervisee. This is where third eye rapport is immensely important.

It is an easy thing to point out that rapport matters. Often, the harder task is to feel it, maintain it and communicate it. So what on earth is the counsellor or supervisor supposed to do? The great majority of people who come for counselling are, at least consciously, co-operative and open and invested in an obvious way in their own change or recovery. Unconsciously they may display a little of what I was describing in these last paragraphs. So, thinking of them, as well as the few people who are more overtly difficult to be with, here are a few of the ways I have seen succeed in making rapport. As supervisor you will keep them in mind when your supervisee is tempting you into the parallel process of acting out some of her counselling session.

One is to keep yourself from being mesmerised. How often have you said, or heard people say that they felt drawn in to a client's game? That is what I call being mesmerised. When I question counsellors closely, I find that those who manage not to stay drawn in or sucked in or mesmerised, have a capacity for looking at their client in a large context.

For example, when someone contradicts, it is possible to tunnel down to a vision of the world which is no bigger than the verbal fight of the moment about who said what, when, and why. Victory is the aim. Your good name or good sense are what you are fighting for. This is an invigorating pastime. It is not always an appropriate one when counselling. Here is a disguised transcript of Claud being counsellor to Maggie, to illustrate what I am saying.

M: [*Lies back in her chair and stretches arms above her head, keeping eye-contact with Claud*] I don't know what to talk about today. [*Smiles*]

C: [*Is aware of feeling sexually aroused. Finds he is grinning back. Now feels alarmed. Maggie is very attractive. Images of throwing himself upon her come to his mind. All this is happening in a nanosecond, but he feels an instant of panic, now imagining headlines in all the tabloid newspapers about him. No longer a psychotherapist, but Psycho The Rapist. All this florid imagining prompts him to draw back, to perceive Maggie and her statement in a larger context than just the intensity of Now. One context is his gestalt training about polarities. He could invite her to explore the polarity, to try out the statement that she does know what she wants to talk about. Her body-posture certainly gives some hints. Another context he goes to, another part of the background, is that Maggie has told of men always chasing her, and her feeling so upset*

*by this that she rejects them forcefully. If he confesses his sexual
feeling, he may sound like these other men. What to do?]* Maggie, I
suggest you tune in to what you want ME to do about your not knowing what
to talk about.

M: [*Easy and flirtatious, rather little girl*] O, I don't know. I
just want you to do it! I don't want to be this responsible grown-up. I want
to be naughty today.

C: Naughty? [*On our video of this session, we both noted in
supervision, as he did all too clearly at the time, that at this point
Maggie put her feet about a foot apart, so that she was lying back
in a way that looked very sexually receptive.*]

M: I do get tired of all this therapy. I'd like to know you in another
way, outside these sessions.

C: I'm curious about how you see this other way of knowing me.

M: O, you know. Just talking and being friends and going for a meal
or something. You're being a bit boring today.

C: I'm looking at how you are sitting, and noticing that you've
crossed your legs as I say that. I remember how you have told me you have
these tantalising encounters with men, and then back off. And that it is
difficult for you to make trusting friendships. I am not going to chase you,
Mary. I am suddenly a bit sad. As if you are lonely, underneath this banter.

MAGGIE: [*Teases*] Boring!

CLAUD: I'm not bored. I'm working hard over here. And I've the
impression that you're putting enormous energy into a game, and not
noticing what the game is about.

This extract is, among much else, about rapport and confluence. It
would have been easy for Claud on one hand to go for confluence, the
apparent rapport of joining in the flirtation. On the other, he might have
felt flustered enough by his own arousal, to button himself into a prim put-
down. But he was secure enough in himself, and loving enough to Maggie,
to stay easy, to fight her as an equal. My belief is that unless that good
feeling had communicated to Maggie, so that she felt trusting of Claud, she
would not have let herself have or admit a painful insight about loneliness,
as she did just afterwards in the session.

Claud moved from the immediate, narrow gestalt, to a larger vision
which took in Maggie's history and the way it was trying to re-enact in the
present. And he moved to a larger and probably more useful truth than the
immediate one of being turned on for a moment by a client.

The foundation of rapport is to learn yourself enough that you know what style you have, and when you are being truthful to yourself. This is much of what training should be about, and it is as well a maintenance task for supervision. You are always changing. In supervision you can comment and even practice some of those changes, with a helpful witness.

At supervision the other day Jim went quiet, then took on a slightly furtive expression.

JIM: *I feel a bit funny saying this. I've taken to not answering my clients sometimes. I feel quite powerful doing it. And it seems to work - I mean they seem to think for themselves, or find what they need to do next. But.*

SUPERVISOR: *But?*

JIM: *Look, I'd like you to talk as if you're Rosemary, the client I was describing just now.*

I agreed, and talked hurriedly, asking my own questions, but in the way he had described Rosemary. Jim's face became pale and pinched, and he drew his lips tight as he looked at me. I stopped role-playing when he raised his hand.

JIM: *I think I've got it. There's so much going on inside me! I'm feeling good about leaving you/Rosemary to answer your own questions. And at the same time I'm feeling really guilty, really bad, at not being nice. And then this defensive, rebellious power feeling, a sort of You-won't-get-me, comes in. It's the lifelong dialogue between my poor hungry yappy Mum, and stern Papa. They're both inside me.*

SUP.: *I'm silent for much of our sessions.*

JIM: *You're different. You're on my side.*

SUP.: *So that sounds like the puzzle. Can you be on your client's side and not answer? Or will you magically turn into Papa the Inspector?*

From this time, Jim began to incorporate into his counselling ways of being encouragingly rather than punitively silent. His good recall of other sessions, his courtesy and attentiveness, were all signals of his good feelings to his clients. In the context of all this, he rightly trusted that his occasional silences could be wise. He stopped needing to purse his lips and turn pale or suffer conflict when he was quiet. He was using supervision to help himself assimilate a change of style, and to be more trusting of himself. As he dropped fear of himself, he could let go of fear of his client. Fear is what underlies almost all failures of rapport.

Another question Jim was grappling with, and that all counsellors need to answer for themselves, was about identity. Was he himself or his father or a portmanteau of both parents? Could he dare answer yes to all three questions? When I hear supervisees protest "But I couldn't do that! It's just not me!" I listen for whether there is panic or self-knowledge in their tone. Are you you when you are talking to the deaf old lady down the road? Doing the conga? Arguing at the supermarket check-out? Picking your nose? Playing ludo with your child? Of course you are. You are whatever you do.

If you are at ease with yourself you will accept this. If you are more fearful, you probably hold on to an image of yourself, to which you try consciously to fit your behaviour, hacking away to make yourself fit this Procrustean bed. Being at ease with yourself is the only position from which you can achieve rapport with anyone else.

Another fact of life is that I and you are always part of a system. The conga is a system, a formalised romp. The supermarket check-out is a system with a role in it for you, that you can play in many ways. You probably need to take far more heed than many counselling courses encourage, in looking at the counselling pair, at you and the client, as a system.

Unless you are very rigid in your personality, in which case you are not very likely to be working in this area, you will be at least subtly different with every person you work with. For a start, you are both talking about, and becoming part of, their life, which is different from every other life in the universe. Much more, you are responding to the countless signals that pass within or without words between you, and in so doing you are spinning a mass of invisible filaments between you, either of bridging, open lines, or of defense. Doing this is probably the most important part of counselling, most of the time. And it is an important element of supervision too. Making a mess of it is, like smoking, dangerous to your health and your client's.

I can recognise myself in each system that I co-create with each supervisee. Yet I feel different and show differently with, say, the woman whose husband was killed when they were on their tenth anniversary holiday; with the young man who told me he was thinking of knifing his flat-mate; with the girl who has just finished her third bout of chemotherapy, and comes to see me in a magnificent turban which covers her baldness. Each dance is a different one.

In supervision too, I and you need to find the ways of being ourselves which communicates with the person supervised, and is effective in helping them with the craft skills of their counselling.

One counsellor I supervise often loses confidence, and gets in a muddle about theory. He came to me wanting to become a shrewd theorist, and for a while I laboured to help him in that direction. But his resistances, or just the way his head is, stopped us in that track. He does what I see as some excellent work with his clients, from the base of his gentleness and intuition.

My job is to help him recognise where he is doing well, to sort out with him what clients he should not see, and to make theoretical issues clear and simple. He seems to learn from the guts upwards, and slowly, surely. With another counsellor, I may dance to a more lively beat. I feel myself speed up in her presence. We have discussions in which we both raise our voices. We laugh often. We both use long words. With both people I feel good rapport, and think I do a good job.

A sense of competence is one reward I get from working with them. Another is that I have found a way of being aspects of myself I enjoy and which seem appropriate, in each system.

USE AND ABUSE OF POWER IN THERAPY

This chapter is taken from part of a talk I gave, with this title. It is included here as a reminder of how complex ethical issues are for counsellor and supervisor alike, and the amount of responsibility that is needed in either role.

MORALITY AND POWER

It is tempting, even reassuring, to assume there are some universal and absolute values for humans. Instead, like the coming and going of geological weather, there are moral climates within and between cultures which change truth itself .

Truth is not something there, that might be found or discovered - but something that must be created and that gives a name to a process, or rather to a will to overcome that has no end - introducing truth, is a process in infinitum, an active determining, not a becoming-conscious of something that is in itself firm and determined.

Nietzsche. (1982)

Foucault (1980) chimes in:

We are all formed and dominated by the values underlying the structure of (our) society.

Truth isn't outside power, or lacking in power... Truth is a thing of this world.....Each society has its regime of truth, its general politics of truth: that is, the general type of discourse which it accepts and makes function as true...(We need also to notice) the status of those who are charged with saying what counts as true.

In counselling this is the place of dilemma. How much is a therapist to uphold the current morality, and how far to question or subvert the status quo? It is easy to swallow whole all sorts of theories as if they were truth.

As Marilyn French (1991) says,

The exculpation of the father, in a psychology that located the formation of character in childhood led directly to the inculpation of the mother. Generations of psychologists have laid the blame for almost all our unhappiness at her tired feet.

At a wider level, mental health itself is as much a cultural artefact as a perceived intrapsychic absolute. Normality and deviance are in great part definitions of what is socially convenient. Adjustment is thus both suspect and desirable: suspect because the social values, the morality-adjusted-to may be bizarre; desirable because social animals need to be in the same ball park as one another. Being too far out of line is distressing to the individual and hard for society, the other people, to tolerate.

To take a few examples, an aversion to loot and pillage presumably made for a bad Viking, as an aversion to stoning adulterous women still means a bad Muslim in certain countries. Incest was your sacred duty in some families in ancient Egypt, as killing is the duty of soldiers in warfare even today.

Counselling cannot be totally outside the morality of the society in which it operates.

Having set the scene by reminding you of the sand, partly the sands-of-time, on which what we call truth is founded, I would like to attempt a definition of power as I understand the word in therapy.

DEFINITIONS OF POWER

Some writers have made an apparently useful distinction between power-to, and power-over. Power-to is ability, the power to make, to give, to do. Power-over is impositional, political. And, with certain exceptions, the power-over of coercion, threat, sanction has no place in therapy. But all tools can be abused, used as weapons. The apparently benign power of empathy, the ability to guess accurately into the world of the other, can soon be used as power over. Or it may be seen as power over by the person who has been accurately guessed. The correct reading of me may lead me or the other to manipulate me, to sell me a second hand car, or devotion to a guru or to one brand of psychological explanation of my character or problem.

Francis Bacon stated that *knowledge itself is power*. Foucault elaborates, suggesting that all compartmentalisation of knowledge is an exercise of power. The creation of a profession, or a particular therapy, is thus the establishment of a power base, which may tempt its adherents to recruit new members to its belief system, and belittle those of other persuasions. This has undoubtedly happened in the field of counselling. I see it as a potential abuse of power by therapists towards patients, if it leads to attempts to chop the patients' psyches to the shape of one or other Procrustean bed of theory.

Human minds need models in order to organise data, to make sense. Models are intrinsically false, however, and need to be recognised as such. Good use of counsellor power, to my mind, is in learning many models. Each has been invented by a theorist with a particular personality or cast of mind, in response to a population of particular personalities or cast of mind, acculturation or history. I become more aware of people who present in what I call a Freudian way, so that perhaps the Oedipal dilemma springs to my mind as I listen. Others, to use a shorthand way of talking here, seem noticeably Kleinian, with splitting the easiest frame of listening for me to hold for a time when I am with them. Knowledge of many theories can at best be power-to, transformative and creative power, leading to power-with the patient.

Many writers have made useful distinctions between power and authority, influence, persuasion and seduction and so forth. But for my purposes, I think of it as something like electricity, electricity that is always turned on. It is a means of illuminating, warming, shocking or even killing. It is energy, physis, life-force in interaction.

In this sense, all relationships are power relationships. Therapist and client assume or assign power, in contest or collaboration. Supervisor and supervisee do likewise.

ETHICS AND POWER

A code of ethics is an abstraction into generality of what was once personal and passionate. At best, ethical codes are a useful shortcut to save us emoting and thinking the same questions over and over. At worst they become a smug justification of alienated behaviour. In a passage I find chilling reading, Foucault arrives at the term *disciplinary power*, the power of a discipline such as counselling or any other. He states that *this is the ordinary form of power by which we can expect to be invaded (in modern times). If the discipline involved finds us a threat to its considered formulae, (its belief system and ethics) we will be attacked or dismissed. If we augment their story, we will be*

*applauded and asked to join. If we do neither, we will be ignored
altogether. In this way, the individual will become progressively
more insignificant.*

He is suggesting that psychotherapeutic institutions can be abusive of
power almost by fact of their existence. Like family rules, their codes of
ethics need to be openly re-justified or replaced in a Maoist continuous
revolution. Keeping out of this dialogue is to my mind an abuse of power by
counsellors and supervisors.

To return to the relationship of therapist to patient, I need here to
put in what is less a value, though it might sound like one, than a description
of reality. As far as I can see, power when it is intentional has two broad
underlying structures. Either it is mediated by fear, or by love. Some
Freudian psychologists see hate as an underlying structure. To me, fear is
before hate; cruelty, spite and vengeance are developments from
underlying fear.

In my view, it then follows that it is ethical for the therapist to put up
whatever boundaries and defences will help her to work without or with
reduced fear, and with proper respect and generosity, or other form of love
which is appropriate. Insofar as I am frightened of the patient, I am likely
to abuse my power towards her.

Most of the time, apparently mundane practicalities are enough to
prevent or reduce fear. Having other people in the building when new
clients or unstable people are there; asking people who manage money
badly to pay in advance; keeping time boundaries, are examples of ethical
enablers of a possibly therapeutic encounter.

Insofar as counselling is a power system, it needs checks and balances
built into it as all power systems do. Regulatory bodies, accreditation,
supervision, continuing study, integrity of life in the counsellor and the
supervisor, are some of the ethical means of making such checks and
balances. Only an informed and compassionate professional body can
where necessary protect the therapist from a patient whose potentially
destructive attacks are a response to history rather than the present. This is
no less and no more important than having clear protective procedures for
the patient who has been abused by a therapist.

Knowing the limits of the relationship with the patient, and having a
clear personal model of the nature of the task of therapy are two large

ethical requirements which are also an aid to completing the energy circuit with the patient in an empowering rather than a power-contest mode.

ROLES IN THE POWER RELATIONSHIP IN THERAPY

I find these three quotations wonderful comment in themselves. They are also contradictory in a way I find salutary.

MACBETH: Canst thou not minister to a mind diseased,
Pluck from the memory a rooted sorrow
Raze out the written troubles of the brain
And with some sweet oblivious antidote
Cleanse the stuffed bosom of that perilous stuff
Which weighs upon the heart?
DOCTOR: Therein the patient must minister to himself.

Then Hippocrates, nearly two and a half thousand years ago:
Some patients, though conscious that their condition is perilous, recover their health simply through their contentment with the goodness of the physician.

Beaumont in The Maid's Tragedy:
They have most power to hurt us that we love.

These statements are a forceful expression of the extraordinary delicacy and power of the counsellor's role. The more I thought about what we do, as I wrote this, the more impossible our profession seemed.

Unhitching a kind of parental ambition for your patient, from your knowledge of what looks possible for him or her, is one of the many occasions when having power over yourself as a counsellor is more important that having power over the other person. Otherwise we are back to competitive power, the will to conquer. Fritz Perls made a fine description of all this as petty victory, the underlying reality of which is self-defeat. He was not making a moralistic point, simply a description of a mechanism. The diagnostic measure of whether I am up to petty victory or informed imposition is the *cui bono*, of whose good is properly being served? It needs to be asked, often.

The counsellor's powers are often best used towards recognising and understanding the world of the patient, and making sense of how that world is or is not being re-created in the present. Only then can self-acceptance and then change take place. Most of the time that holds good, in my experience. But it does not when dealing with some people, specially when they are in extreme agitation. I have sometimes found that the only useful, calming interventions to someone in a manic state have been prescriptive and proscriptive. "No, Mary, I don't want you to drive to Edinburgh tonight and fetch your children out of school. I want you well enough to be peacefully at home when their holiday comes." When I have said such things, I have honestly done so with the clear sense that my wanting does not constitute a command. But the words are arguably a monstrous imposition, taking away from the patient all her responsibility for herself.

I have seen the power-exchange differently. Telling me a series of potentially catastrophic actions she was about to take was, I think, the last squeak for help that Mary could muster. It would to my mind have been as callous to remind her at such a point that she was captain of her soul and mistress of her fate, as to tell someone who has been knocked down by a car that they have chosen their actions, so the consequences of those actions must be their choice too. Whether or not this philosophising has any truth in it, the survival chances of either of these people is poor without very active intervention by others. This is one of the possible advantages of belonging as we do to a social species. We help each other.

As counsellors and as supervisors we have constantly to refine our judgement about the point at which help itself becomes crippling, and turns to dysfunctional power over the other.

We need a kind of dogged honesty and simplicity, and the humility to see denigration or idealisation of us by the patient in a far wider context than just transactions at ourselves. In systems language, we need often to shift the focus of contest or struggle from ourselves, to what Macbeth called the disease, the dis-ease. That is the enemy for patient and therapist and supervisor to unite their powers to overcome.

Love is involved in this, and a progressive casting out of fear. A vast proportion of the errors therapists tell me they have committed can be traced back to fear. Fear of the assault of the patient; fear of not knowing; fear of losing face; fear of losing control; fear of the material the patient presents.

The task of the patient is massively different. She has no duty of truthfulness, honesty, as we have. Some of the time, she will be doing a good job in giving a florid display of her dysfunctional behaviours to, or more likely at, the counsellor. Provocatively, I could say that her work is at times to do her utmost to abuse power, her own and the counsellor's. The counsellor's task is to do her utmost to prevent that abuse, and to work towards power-with.

As a supervisor I am often faced with a counsellor who is aggrieved because the patient is not playing the therapy game according to her or his expectations. The walk-out, the insult, the morose silence, the apparent amnesia about last week's careful work, can be hard to understand or respond to in a way that will be useful to both parties. Good use of power is to work towards that functional response, and to acknowledge the reactive anger or vengeance or despair that surface in the counsellor's mind as comments on the reactions that patient probably elicits in many other scenes besides the present.

Sinking into hurt before a patient who is wanting to hurt, or in many other ways becoming part of what is essentially one of the dysfunctional intrapsychic dialogues of the patient, is an abuse of power *by the counsellor.* Supervision is often the necessary enlightener to keep this from happening to any grave degree.

The therapist's major task, often, is to configure a wider scene, a larger gestalt, than the patient does. Elsewhere I have described this as having third eye rapport.

Tout comprendre, c'est tout pardonner. Well, it is not given to any of us to understand everything. But we can at least be in what Buber (1970) calls the one-sided dialogic stance, which in part I take to mean, having goodwill towards understanding, and goodwill towards the other person, along with an open acceptance and easiness about the phenomena of your own responses.

That to me is the proper use of power by the therapist. Like actors we are the instruments we work with. Actors are to give a representation of truth. Therapists are to be truthful. Contextual awareness is the major part of that truthfulness. The patient is likely to spend an exceedingly small proportion of her time with us, however significant that time becomes. Responding to her needs for convalescence, perhaps, or active investigation group, an illusory cocoon of goodness in a bad world, is likely to be abusive of her in the long term, just as much as if I let myself into the sniping or despairing co-creation of reality that she might beaver away to make me join in.

Counselling is a response to this society. I saw a piece in the paper lately claiming that it did no more good than a chat with a friend, and thought sadly, when I had got over my first defensive hump, that maybe we are only here because there have been widespread failures of friendship. We have not been taught the art of it. I wish that children in school were regularly allowed tuition and practice in human relationship. They respond amazingly to such learning where I have seen it happening.

To my mind, one of the best uses of the very beautiful and remarkable insight and power that I see my supervisees and other counsellors cultivating, to be in the prophylactic work of education. There is a risk that our profession might otherwise in the long term be abusive of our society. If we corner love and understanding, we may keep ourselves in work, but at the same time deprive what Ivan Illich (1973) calls the laity.

KEEPING RECORDS

Enough people who come to me for supervision have had problems with writing up sessions, to warrant writing at some length about the nitty-gritty of recording individual and group sessions.

If you see very few clients, and are comparatively fresh to counselling, I do believe that you may carry full and clear memories of what they and you are doing in your sessions, without any writing up. However, that memory will not last too long in its springlike freshness. It is highly unlikely to last even with that client, if you go on seeing her for some months. It will certainly not last with clarity when you have moved on to other people.

What you need minimally, therefore, is a clear record of what happened when. A discipline for this bottom-line task is to imagine that you might be called into court to give evidence of your patient's whereabouts and state of mind on any of those dates when she was seeing you. You might be. Now let yourself imagine two more scenes. One is of your client having some kind of breakdown, and asking you to talk with her doctor or psychiatrist. The last is of your client making a good ending of counselling with you, and saying in the last session, "By the way, I know you keep notes on me. I should rather like to have a look at them, or keep them."

The answer to this last might for some counsellors be no, though some codes of ethics stipulate that clients' notes must be available to them. What I am suggesting is that you keep your notes in such a way that you can give an unflummoxed answer to whatever questions are asked concerning them.

If you are as resistant as I can be to writing up notes properly, you will do well to make the task as inviting as possible, first by having ready appropriate writing materials. A large exercise book for each client is an investment some people find worthwhile. Another writing-up device which works well for many people is to take a new sheet of loose-leaf paper for each session. Different-coloured folders for different clients give me a sense of good cheer and of being in charge, which I certainly need to cultivate by whatever slight means are around.

Next, you may do well to have a schema for writing up, which keeps you from rambling, and helps you include what is going to be most useful when you look back at your notes. Here are some ways that work, for you to copy or adapt if you have not already settled on a method which suits you.

FACTS LEFT

You can use the left hand page for writing down when your client saw you, whether she was late or early, whether her payments are up to date, what you did about it, what you talked about or did, and how you ended. The right hand page is a written version of what Patrick Casement (1985) calls The Internal Supervisor. On it, either as you go along, or later, you write in your feelings, hunches, opinions and reminders to yourself, and a reminder of any theme you want to focus on next time. At the bottom of the page you may want to note whatever you want to talk over with your supervisor.

MARGIN PAGE

However you divide what you are putting down, using a two-page spread can be clarifying. A very simple way is just to use the right hand page as an extended margin. On the left you write down everything you want to record. Then you read back, and as extra memories, or comments and ideas, come up in your mind, you put them opposite the relevant parts of the notes on the left.

ME RIGHT

If you suspect that you can get too identified with your clients, you may like to keep the left hand page for the client, and the right hand one for you. For clarity, it can help to offset what you write. So, if you start on the left with five lines quoting from or telling about your client, then you start writing at line six on the right, to describe your response. Then you switch back to the left below where you stop writing on the right, and so on.

BRACKETS

The data of the session and the commentary may be interwoven, perhaps with brackets round the commentary, to indicate that you know when you are recording data and when you are surmising. Or you may prefer to rule a line down the middle of the sheet, and use the left and right sides as I have suggested already.

COLOURS

Using a different coloured pen for overwriting different kinds of comment is another simple device which makes clear what you were doing, even when you return to the notes months later.

RECORDING SESSIONS WITH GROUPS

There is such an enormous amount of material generated in any group, that you will only be aware of a limited part of it, and will openly deal openly with a faction of that limited part.

Nevertheless, you will *set* yourself at least to hold awareness of all the group members. The Gestalt way of doing this is often via the Significant Missing Element. That is to say, you can probably accustom yourself to getting a jolt from time to time as you realise that this or that person, sub-group or even majority has in fact slipped out of your awareness for longer than is comfortable. That gap of awareness has learning in it about where you were influenced or chose to focus. It says something about the whole group, too.

This is a concrete starting place for reminding yourself that the field of the whole group, (or more, sometimes) is the ground on which any person or interaction becomes figural. If you find that in your note-writing you are voluminous about one episode, then check if you have got dazzled by a figure. What is the relation of that figure to the whole group or other parts of the group? What does that interaction represent in terms of that group? Is it a dramatisation or allegory of a repeating story here? Is it an attempt to get away from a prevailing ethos? Does it relate to belonging and its polarity of quitting? Does it relate to control and its polarity, yielding or passivity?

Most of these questions are connected to your readiness to hold what I call a Wide Gestalt, both across the present of the group, and through its history. That is where every happening is embedded, as in a matrix. What you need in your perception and your record-keeping is the ability to let associations form, memories nest together, images surface, so that you acknowledge the co-creation that happens.

In reading some student notes of groups, I reckon that the ground is the student's anxiety about whether she is making good responses to individuals. That has importance. What I am also stressing is that you look for the tendency, the emerging process, rather than the isolated event. For example, it is rarely important in group notes to give a long account of one piece of work with one person. What may need noting is how that work relates to the rest of what is going on, or perhaps, how the protagonist finished, in terms of being fulfilled or frustrated. In other words, the intrapsychic in a group sits alongside the interpersonal and the systems levels of intervention and awareness.

Individual intrapsychic work in a group may provoke a queue of people interested in doing the same, and thereby neglecting the other levels of experience. As supervisor you need to know both if this is happening, and if it is, whether the worker understands and is satisfied with the dynamic provoked.

FOCUS

If you as staff member or supervisor do not know what the group is for or what you hope from it, you are unlikely to write with any focus of awareness, or any criterion for evaluating what is happening. Is it for therapy, social skills learning, support, process awareness, counselling theory and practice? Having a sure answer makes a good starting place for work and for writing up.

ECONOMY OF WRITING

By paying attention to the Wide Gestalt, you help your supervisee make overall sense of the group, rather than sticking in a bog of detail. You may do well asking the question *What was this about?* rather than just *What Happened?* The answer may suggest some new angle for addressing and writing up the next session. The supervisee may focus for one week on seeing what happens in terms of, say, Bion (1961), or Stern (1985).

She may find great richness in staying with some image produced by one of the group in a session, and construing in terms of that. A swimming pool is a common (and hopeful) image someone might use. She might tell herself enough in her notes by expanding the image, noting who stayed on the brink, plunged in and so forth, and whether she herself seemed like a lifeguard or hydrophobic.

GROUP RECORDING DEVICES

As supervisee, over a number of sessions you may like to vary how you record. Here are one or two possibilities. You may think of more or better.

SUBBING

Finding headings and sub-headings for what you put on paper is often a way of clarifying the theme, mood or concept that you need to keep in focus. As well as some form of historical account, as I have talked of here, you may do some audio or visual taping if the group agrees, and use PPR and notes.

PRE-SELECTION

For one session you may focus on one element, for example mostly on the interaction between you and a co-worker, commenting that in terms of the effect on the group and vice versa. Justify to yourself the element you choose, so that you know if you still have the Wide Gestalt, or are just disappearing into something familiar and perhaps mildly irrelevant.

GRID

Making a grid can be informative. The names of the members are written down the side. Time is marked off across the top. You can devise your own symbols to show the different sorts of activity that you are noticing, and fill them in in the appropriate squares. This mechanistic model is a help to improving overall awareness, and may teach you what you need to focus on in further meetings.

INTERACTION DIAGRAM

Draw a large circle with people's names where they sat. Fill in lines to denote interactions, again with whatever colours or ciphers you want to denote different intensity or quality of engagement. You can ask members of the group to fill this out, as feedback to themselves as well as a help to you.

INDIVIDUAL CONTRIBUTION RECORD $\left(\text{NB } \overline{\text{for supervision}}\right)$ Babs, 444 4

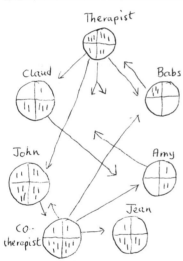

Each personal circle may be divided into time quartiles, and a note made of when they intervened least and most. If as supervisor you observe a group, it is easy to put a 1 by the name of each person who speaks in the first quartile, a 2 for the second, and so forth. Interaction lines can be put in at the same time. This gives good background data for the supervision session you will have later with the people who led the group.

ZOOM

Where you record in a schematic way, with diagrams, you may choose to zoom in on one or two episodes for more extensive notes. Again, notice what makes you choose.

THE CAREER EVOLUTION OF INDIVIDUAL OR GROUP NOTES

As a student you need to keep fuller and probably more laborious notes than you will later in your career. In training you are likely to have written verbatim recalls of sessions, for example. Perhaps you did not, but just made sound or video records, from which you wrote extracts with commentaries. Both these useful devices are very time-consuming. From time to time, though, they are an important part of supervision in later life, giving you and your supervisor a chance to see if you play as good a game as you talk: reporting aloud often blurs some of the clumsinesses, the odd sloppy habit you acquire in the privacy of your one-to-one session.

At student stage, there is much to be said for making space in your notes, at least from time to time, for reminders of what was behind what you said. Put in other words, this means the theoretical justification for what you uttered. At a simple level, you may come to realise that you have fallen into some habit like asking far too many questions. Or you may have taken to being what you liked to think was empathic, but sounds on reflection more like collusive.

As you become more experienced, you may come to know how much detail you need to keep in your notes.

How much are you going to write? Consult yourself. You know if you are inclined to be laborious, and sit over writing jobs, hating them and elongating them, all at the same time. Do you need to? Talk to your supervisor about it. Or are you clever and quick and scatter-brained, and get by because, at least as far as you can remember, you have an excellent memory? Whatever your personality, you need to find a way of writing up that suits you, that lets you monitor yourself, and that does justice to the work your client is doing in the sessions.

MINIMUM EFFORT FOR MAXIMUM USEFULNESS.

If you ask people to tell their history at some length when they first come to you, this circumstantial information about them will inevitably be at the beginning of your notes, easily accessible when you falter in your memory of how many siblings they have, or whether their father died or ran off when they were two. Many counsellors, specially if they work for short times with people, do not begin like this. To them I recommend keeping space at the beginning of the file or notebook, in which to record the client's family history, stated reason for coming to counselling, and the counsellor's view of the most useful focus.

The headings in this section could be

1. NAME [probably coded] AND MEANS OF CONTACT

*2. PRESENT CIRCUMSTANCES [Mrs A is 28, living since she was
eighteen with Claud. Works at Boots.]*

*3. HISTORY [Leave plenty of room to note in facts about her life
and her ways of dealing with its events]*

*4. REASON FOR SEEING ME [Has changed jobs three times in
the last few months, and thinks she is unreasonably difficult with
everyone at work, though she gets on perfectly, her word, with
family and Claud]*

*5. MY HUNCHES [She said strongly out of the blue that she was
not thinking of leaving work and having a baby. I guess she is.
Longer-term work probably about her daring to acknowledge her
own needs, and admit the humanness of close family, and therefore
self.]*

*6. TIMES AND PAYMENTS [Tuesdays at 11am, with 3-week
break at Easter when she will be abroad. One month paid in
advance, next payment due...]*

SECURITY

Find a set place
for your notes, where you
always keep them unless
you are using them.

At best this is a locked file drawer. If you keep your records on an
open shelf, then I advise that you use no more than an initial to denote your
client, and you keep his or her full details elsewhere.

I can tell several hair-raising anecdotes to justify this advice. One is
of a jobbing builder reading the counselling notes about his sister-in-law's
marital problems. These were apparently lying in a named folder on a
window-sill. Another is of a disturbed client's deliberately stealing the
notes, again in a named folder, about her friend [and enemy] who came to
the same counsellor. Another is of police coming to the flat where a

counsellor had a room, with a search warrant which had nothing to do with the counsellor. But her files were taken away. Do all of these stories sound as if they could not possibly happen to you? I'm glad if it's true. What might go wrong in your case, then? Think about it and take precautions. In good counselling, clients show the substance of themselves, their fears and secrets and pain and irrationality and hope. They give you the power, very often, to destroy their good name. Shakespeare had pertinent things to say about that.

INVENTING A DRILL

Making a habit of keeping notes is an aid to good practice, good learning, and peace of mind. You have the materials, with some spare for the new people who come along. You have a place to keep the records. Last, designate a time when you do your writing up, within 24 hours of the session. Straight afterwards is an excellent time, if you can manage it. Late at night suits others. Just be clear about your own method, and stay with it. Counselling needs to be a rigorous profession, even if you do it for no money, for few sessions a week. Nowhere is that rigour more needed than in steadily holding to a discipline of note-keeping.

As a counsellor, I rarely look forward with any pleasure to writing up. Then when I begin, I am often fascinated. As a supervisor, I will not accept anyone as supervisee unless she or he is willing to write notes, and occasionally write up a verbatim report of part of a session, for us to talk over together. In making that requirement, I am thinking of the people who are counselled. They deserve our trouble.

SUPERVISOR'S NOTES

I know supervisors who do not keep any notes. I know others who keep fairly complete accounts of their supervisees' sessions. I am averse to keeping records of what is third hand, that is to say, the supervisee's client's life-story. The notes that the supervisee brings along with her will tell me, or should tell me, as much as I need to know about all that.

What I need to keep in focus, and in my note file, is what I am observing about the supervisee herself. This may sound dreadfully obvious to you. But I have been astonished on many occasions to find supervisors simply and solely joining in with the counsellor as another commentator of the client's problems.

My supervision notes are much briefer than therapy notes. They contain details of dates, times, payment, for everyone. Then for newer supervisees I write more about their mood and manner, way of working, and possible gaps in their skills. With people I have known much longer, I jot down their theme, and a brief record of who they were talking about. Supervision notes will also contain the record of review sessions, or of my requests for verbatim recording or whatever. The notes show me whether a supervisee wants to spend many sessions talking on and on about one client, or tries to skitter like a pond-skater over problem points with six clients, every session.

By generally giving one page to each session, I can make the exercise book I use for each supervisee into a bring-forward file, reminding myself under future dates to ask particular questions, or ask about some difficult work, or new piece of training.

Notes are a surer check than memory, that over a period you are acknowledging all the people the supervisee sees, and are keeping a balance in how we do that. However full or abbreviated they are, you need to keep clarity about what is data and what is guess or inference.

SKIN RELATION

Physical contact between supervisee and supervisor, and between counsellor and client, has in my experience become yet more taboo in the five years since this was first written. This is not at all surprising, given that those relationships are likely to generate strong implicit intimacy, a kind of dry grass of the emotions, ready to burst into fire if one spark falls.

All codes of ethics and practice that I have read, are strict about the avoidance of sexual contact or innuendo between counsellor and client. And quite right too. Touch can be the spark to that tinder, thus it is often advised against.

I want to stay clear in my own mind that much good counselling, and a strong strand of supervision, amount to an elaborate symbolisation of simple touch. What is sometimes called containment is at some moments the equivalent of holding the client on your lap until she feels comforted enough to be cramped there, and want to get down. The supervisor's attitude in much of a session might be sculpted as standing with an arm round the shoulder of the supervisee, who leans against her for the moment, feeling valued enough as the two people look together at her work, for her to make yet more sense of it than she did when sitting alone.

Touch is the more potent as we outlaw it, and this makes it more politic for supervisors and counsellors to keep vigilant about its use.

Political expediency and truthful action are scarcely synonyms. Although we give more potency by taboos, touch is intrinsically of vast significance and nurturing value to humans. It is our first interpersonal communication, the very expression of early care and love, and of nourishment. [There is a large ethical question for supervisors and counsellors here, as to whether they make strict easily observable rules against it, or work awarely and painstakingly towards a cultural shift.]

I remember Harlow's experiments with monkeys, specially that in which young monkeys were exposed to wire netting mother-shapes which contained perfectly good milk, and cloth mother shapes, similarly equipped. It took that experiment to remind many people of what the rest had always intuited - that monkeys, and probably people, respond far better to some comfort and warmth than to coldness and discomfort.

Very many of the people who turn up for counselling have been through some version of the wire-netting monkey experience. Yet the counsellor may well be chary of turning into no more than temporary cloth mothers for them.

My mind is running on animals. I think of the pleasantness of having a cat sit on my knee, and the uncomfortable reflection that goes along with that; by stroking and cuddling cats, we literally infantilise them. They act like kittens, asking for fondling and grooming, because we step in right where their mothers left off, and keep them for the rest of their lives as part-baby. It is possible to do something like that with humans. At this point I think of a recent and pitiful set of experiments with chimpanzees, in which the young were variously deprived of contact. Those kept away from their mothers completely for a certain period became totally anti-social, responding to all attempts at contact with attack, and generally behaving like juvenile delinquents. Autopsy showed a withering of part of their brain.

The inference is that something as drastic probably can happen to humans. What is emotional is physiological. Such are our powers, however, shown in the extraordinary recovery people sometimes make after brain damage, by transferring the abilities of one frontal lobe to the other, that it is worth, in my view, assuming that re-learning of love, of social behaviour and its pleasures is possible.

What makes me speak at such length of all this is in part as a reminder of the enormous effect people have on each other, every moment, when we are in, and when we are apparently out of, contact. The contact the client has with a counsellor, and that we have as supervisor and counsellor, undoubtedly and demonstrably have direct measurable physical effects on us all. Physical. I am not talking just in some vague area of vibes and fancies, but directly of body chemistry: of health.

There are schools of counselling which favour a certain remoteness in the counsellor. At worst this can be wire-netting relating - offering excellent milk, in the form of correct diagnosis and comment, but modelling the emotional starvation which has perhaps characterised the client's world for much of his or her life.

At the other end of the scale are those whose practitioners sometimes behave as if smiling, cosy, smother-mothering or daddy-hugging constitute helpful behaviour. At worst this manipulates the client into being a domestic cat, or else into getting-better-for Daddy or Mummy, or feeling bad for failing to. It induces dependent feelings beyond the real dependence there is in the relation between counsellor and counselled, or supervisor and supervised.

The social taboos and fears around touching are all, insofar as I have traced them with many people, to do with sex and violence. When I am working as a counsellor, I rarely touch people during a one-to-one session. Sometimes I put a hand on their arm as they leave. Touch is so potent that I do not want to rouse the amount of hope or of fear, or the impulsive responses, or the suppressed impulses, that might result. I feel shy of touch, one-to-one, with people who have come to me because they are not feeling as put-together as they want to.

In a group I feel and behave differently. The presence of other people seems to help make clear that I am not making a threat, or sexual advances to someone when I touch their hand or head or whatever. And the presence of other people also assures me that I am not likely to be swiped by the person touched, who may associate intimacy and violence, to the point of panic response. In a group, I may touch a number of people at different times. So it is clear that I am not setting up an exclusive pairing with anybody. One to one, this would not be demonstrable.

But social mores around feeling are changing in some respects. Crying is far less derided among men than was true twenty years ago. Holding therapy for autistic children has been shown on television. Little by little, I imagine, people who spend more of their working hours dissociated from physical contact, sitting at their lonely computer terminals, will balance this alienation with more literal ways of being in contact, than just keying in to the Internet. They will look for dance and movement and sitting close, and generally being in touch with other humans.

Some trained practitioners spend much of their therapy or counselling sessions in movement, and use far fewer words than I do. Massage is probably more common now than some years ago. Touch is being legitimised in some professional settings, at best within strict codes of conduct. As a supervisor you need to know both what is right for you, and where you are tolerant of other people's practice, and where your own scare gets in the way of accepting different methods from your own.

The only rules I have come up with for myself are the same as in other aspects of supervision. I require honesty of the counsellor. From time to time a supervisee reports to me that a client asked for some physical contact which she gave, though knowing she did not want to. That is not honest.

Emma reported having a male client who asked her to hold his hand for almost half the session. She had done so, but unwillingly.

S: *You are recoiling a little as you tell this.*

E: *He gripped my hand, squashing my fingers.*

S: *So you were letting him have you in his grip.*

E: *It felt like that, as if he had the power. (She experiments with her own hands with different grips) Touching palms, or holding the solid part of my hand, would feel like warmth. That finger-squash just made me angry, sort of alienated and overpowered. And I was getting an ache in my shoulder from stretching across.*

S: *I am playing with the idea of that moment as a sculpt of some of your work with him, and too of what you have told me of his relation with his girlfriend.*

E: *And she just seems to put up with him! I shall comment and refuse next time, instead of colluding.*

It had not taken long for Emma to see that her client was probably intent on rather literally getting the upper hand with her, as he said he did in much of his life. Not touching at that moment might lead to more learning than a dishonest response could.

More complicated, to my mind, is the sad client who wants comfort. When someone already known to the counsellor has arrived at a session with the news of the death of a child or other close friend or relative, I have sometimes felt the counsellor was much more useful to that person, in simply holding them and letting them cry, than trying to talk into their overwhelming emotion.

Then with others, who are not in a particular crisis, I have suspicions that their low feelings are a victim racket, aimed at making the counsellor rescue them from reality. I become much more interested in the structure of what is going on between the two, than the specifics of what the client is saying. I am more concerned with finding out why she wants to cast the counsellor as cuddler, than in doing any cuddling. The relation with them, after all, is bounded very clearly by time and money. Maybe the counsellor has only spent four or five hours in their company, ever, at that point. Is he or she trying to turn the counsellor into The One Person Who Really Understands? Is she being invited into collusive beatification? Help.

Perhaps the counsellor will be of more real use if she shows her boundaries, and prevents an oozing into parent-child or lover-like relating.

GUIDE-LINES

* *Never initiate contact without checking in words if it is all right to do so.*

* *If invited into physical contact, find your honest response and talk about it, whether it is a yes or no, whether you have a hug or just sit there. Relate what is going on to other parts of the client's life than just this moment.*

* *Slip outside yourself for a half-second and look at the system. What do you look as if you're doing, from the internal monitor or supervisor position? What do you look like from the client's position?*

* *Talk about the contact. Keep it in the foreground rather than having it as an apparently ignored activity.*

With many of the supervisees I see, who are working alone a great deal, I let myself kiss them or hug them in greeting or farewell, and feel the better for it. I also check with them whether they are transferring this way of going on to their clients, and whether they feel that that is proper. I do not suggest that you should hug your supervisees. You may roll your eyes to Heaven at the thought. Well, see what that is about. Check that you are not covertly training them to coldness. If not, then all seems fine.

Some supervisees justify physically showing their good feelings to their clients, with some of the arguments I have used in relation to them. People who come to counselling are often at a vulnerable transition in their lives. Reminding them of the simplicity and economy of effort in an embrace is good modelling, say these counsellors.

I am not out to convert supervisees to do all the same things that I do. But in this as in any other exchange, I ask the supervisee to check whether she is helping the client into being better at living, or whether she is setting up the Garden of Eden, and making the counselling sessions a substitute for life, for the client, and even for herself. The splitters, the people Melanie Klein (1952) perceived so vividly, can have a great time with a counsellor who will join in with a game of being all-good or all-bad.

That gives the splitter a chance to cast her spouse, family, maybe the rest of the world, in an opposite role. In such a case the counsellor is helping the client create unreality.

I often feel suspicious of physical contact in counselling which is not acknowledged in words. If a client wants a hug from my supervisee, then the supervisee knows that she is not violating that person's kinosphere in giving it. But I want her also to ask the client,

"Who else do you hug? Who hugs you?" I want her to critique the hug. One hug can be a complete dissertation on how that person gets on with people. Is she a flopper on to your shoulder, a clinger who won't let go? Is she stiff as a board, snatching you to her upper half for a second, then pushing you off? Does she go in for an enveloping writhe that results in you feeling sexy?

What feelings does she give herself as she hugs you? There is a great deal to find out about a hug, or anything else, if the counsellor is encouraged to do her job properly, and actually notice and comment what goes on in the session, rather than just go along with it.

When I first wrote this chapter, I imagined looking at it again in ten or twenty years time. At the beginning of this revision I have commented the greater strictness I fancy, which connects with the tendency to regulation in so many parts of life, from the size of apples to the position of the washing-machine in a private house, to the proper regulatory mechanisms embodied in complaints procedures against many professionals. The present corollary of this last is that alongside the serious complaints that need action, some frivolous or malicious ones are brought. And that is likely to make many warm-hearted people more circumspect than they might like to be in a clinical setting.

I shall be content if after a time what I have written seems out of date, because people have returned to greater easiness than most of us have now about touching each other. If Victorian values win, however, then I suppose that touch will still for many people be fraught with sexual unease, and, alas, what I have written may still apply.

GETTING MOVING

Much of the time of individual supervision is well used in giving the supervisee space to reflect aloud, and in raising her awareness by often phenomenological commentary. The intensity of this often quiet exchange is sometimes less suitable for the entire time in supervision groups.

When a group of trainee counsellors filled in a questionnaire for me about supervision, an activity within sessions that most of them rated highly was role-play. I was not surprised. Any way of learning that involves some movement and imagination seems to me an improvement on just sitting on your bottom for the whole of a session.

In this chapter I shall describe a few ways, beyond the conventionally verbal, of working with supervisees. In case it is unfamiliar to you, I first give an example of a particular way of setting up supervision role play in supervision groups.

JO: I've started seeing this couple, Larry and Lil, and I feel totally out of my depth. They seem to loathe each other and loathe me, and they interrupt the whole time. I can't honestly see why they come.

After a little more talk, Jo decides that he would like a role play, as a way of giving himself more insight and grasp, and with luck some ideas for going forward. He picks Tom and Trish to play the couple, to which they agree.

S: Place them and their chairs the way they tend to sit in the session. [He puts two chairs for them, facing away from each other at about forty five degrees; group members laugh and exclaim]

JO: I've never even commented that to them, the way they won't look at each other. They walk in going hammer and tongs..

S: [Interrupts] Settle for the role play, or have a good old winge. Not both at once. Which?

JO: Role play.

S: Start by standing behind Trish with your hands on her shoulders. Talk in the first person, describing yourself as if you are the wife, Lil. If Trish wants to find out more about Lil, she

asks questions, also in the first person. Lil is the subject for the
moment.

JO: *My name's Lil. I'm 38. My father divorced my mother*
when I was two, and she married a man who didn't like me.

TRISH: *Does my voice really sound like that?*

JO: [Heightens his voice a little and purses his mouth] *I tend to*
shoot out a lot of words like a machine gun, then clamp my mouth
shut. [Keeping this style, he tells more about lil, always in the first person]

TRISH: *What's my feel of myself, my underlying emotion?*

JO: *I feel pretty hard done by. Angry. I'd better fight my*
corner or I'll go down. [Jo breaks off to comment] *I hadn't sensed*
that properly before - the isolated feeling of having to keep lashing
out or else be overwhelmed.

S: *That may be a very accurate guess. But it's only a guess.*
You look as if you're making a useful hypothesis. Keep going.

He and Trish work on in the same way for a few minutes, so that both
have a fair sense of Lil as Jo sees or intuits her. Then he does the same
exercise with Tom, cast as Larry. From time to time other people in the
group ask questions of Jo-as-Larry or Jo-as-Lil. The questions are aimed to
help Jo see more about his clients or his response to them. The questions
are not merely to gratify the group member's curiosity. I make sure that all
the questions are directly to the roles, so that a rambling About session
does not set in.

NICK: [To Jo who is standing with his hands on Tom's shoulders]
Larry, does Lil have nice legs?

S: [Suspicious] *What do you ask that for?*

NICK: *I've a guess around sexual teasing in this marriage.*

JO: *You're right.*

S: *Talk in character in a role-play; don't talk about.*

JO: [As Larry] *She's got film star legs. I like her to wear*
seamed stockings.

As this exercise goes on, Jo enlarges his sense of the people he is
working with; other group members are involved and can add their
enquiries; and Tom and Trish are learning a good deal about the characters
they will role play in a few minutes.

Next, the supervisor asks Jo, Tom and Trish to imagine themselves in
next week's counselling session. Predictably, Tom and Trish soon have the
bit between their teeth, and are galloping into virtuoso performances of the

dominant couple, while Jo opens and shuts his mouth, much in the manner of an expiring codfish. The scene is stopped as soon as the supervisor thinks the manner of it has really struck everyone enough.

Now another group member takes Jo's place, so he can sit and watch, instead of being out there as a protagonist. She soon flounders, at which point she says loudly,

"*Doubles all round!*" In this group, this phrase has come to be the cipher to allow all group members to participate. What they are now licenced to do is stand behind any of the characters in the role play, with hands on their shoulders, and speak whatever lines they deem it likely or important that that character utters, whether or not the words might be available to that person in reality. As soon as they have said their say, they sit down in the circle again.

Tom, Trish and Jo, or by now the counsellor who has taken his place, continue their dialogue, incorporating the statements for which they have acted as mediums. If the statements did not engage them, they carry on as they wish. In this way, much easier to do than to describe, a composite view of what is happening between Jo and his clients can be expressed and worked on in a direct experiment, rather than talked about.

Some group members have an inkling of more of the subtext, the unspoken statements, under the couple's tart quarrelsomeness. Others have their own ideas of effective ways of intervening, and speak from the counsellor place.

The supervisor's job here has something of stage director in it. It is up to her to interrupt creatively. Just letting a scene run down till people are tired and repetitive is usually much less useful than stopping whenever what looks like a telling point is made, and creating space for it to be mulled over.

When the role play itself is over, time is needed to let Jo, or whoever is seeking help, talk through some of his learning. He will need to reject some ideas openly, to question others, to remind himself where he easily falters or loses courage, where his own patterns mesh too easily with those of his clients. In this talk afterwards, the experience of the other actors, and the rest of the group, is likely to be illuminating to Jo and to the members themselves.

As at most times in supervision, good feeling between the participants is important. Without it, Jo might not have wanted to confess his feelings of incompetence in the first place, let alone with such open self-derision. During the exercise there is certainly quite lively group competition to find the deepest insight or the neatest intervention. It seems to me to work best when that competition is sensed by everyone to happen on a raft, a substructure, of good will towards Jo or whoever has put himself in a vulnerable position.

On occasion I have noticed that a group member who is not only very bright, but is a smart Alec, may produce excellent comment, which the group then ignores. There is something for everyone to learn at such moments, about hostility and resistance. Most of the time, the group works far more effectively if love and co-operation, as well as hostility and competitiveness, are openly present and recognised.

Now here is a briefer non-verbal method, which can be an extension of role play, or be used to illuminate something about the system of counsellor and client that the supervisee is presenting.

STRIKING ATTITUDES

Attitude is physical. Attitude dictates or reflects role.

"O. I know what she would do now! She'd lean right over and stare at her feet." or whatever, may prompt insight into the client's patterned way of regulating intimacy, or of suppressing conflict. These memories which become forecasts are an important part of the dialogue. The body movements of *both* parties have a large unconscious effect on the exchanges in the counselling room.

Think of it for yourself. If you know that when you mention fish and chips, or fathers, or mountain-climbing, the person opposite you is going to slide down the chair and shut her eyes, or start·tapping her foot, that is very likely to have an effect on the subjects you bring into the conversation.

As you well know, these peculiar little dances or power-plays are rarely mentioned, and rarely brought out much into awareness in ordinary social exchanges. They may be ciphers, representations of somebody's recurrent way of dealing with experience. A counselling role play is an excellent opportunity to investigate the effect of such behaviour on the counsellor, whether it is her attitude or her client's. Very often, the words tune the behaviour is out of the counsellor's awareness.

To sum up, I recommend that in any piece of role play, attention, which does not necessarily mean much time, is given to all the physical aspects of enactment that I have just described, as well as to the compensating attitudes of the counsellor: in short, to the system which is physically portrayed by the two.

If the counsellor, in a group, seems to have a blind spot about some physical habit of her own, she may be willing to let other supervisees demonstrate it to her. Video will do the same work, less participatively.

THE VIGNETTE

Very often a piece of role play supervision is best ended with a vignette. From what the supervisee has learned, she sets up a final short scene in which she reminds herself once more of a new possibility, a way of breaking an old habit, or whatever has salience for her at that moment.

Role play in one to one supervision cannot be of just this kind. The only combinations available are that the supervisor plays client, or counsellor, with the supervisee taking the complementary roles. Both these exercises make for vividness and change of pace, and generally advance learning. My practice is, if we use role play, to take the part of the client first. I shall certainly know enough already about the client I am playing, not to need a formal hands-on-shoulders introduction like the one I suggested for group supervision. From the client place, I can see for myself just where the counsellor falters, or where, perhaps, she is doing fine but misdoubting herself.

I am sometimes less willing to play the counsellor, particularly with supervisees I suspect of laziness. I do not want to hand them a set of ready-made interventions to carry away and serve up to their client, irrespective of what that poor person is thinking and talking about. I have known such things happen.

By and large, if a supervisee says in a wistful or wheedling voice that she would so like to know what I would say in this or that circumstance, I take care not to oblige. On the other hand, working with competent counsellors who have come across an old blind spot of their own, or a client whose behaviour they are not yet making sense of, I let myself play counsellor for a two or three-minute demonstration that we can then talk over.

Both are important, the experiment and the time for reflection. The role play may give an immediate insight. The talking over, chewing over, gives an opportunity for assimilating the learning into the counsellor's whole way of working. In other words, role play starts off as an ad hoc way of tackling a particular difficulty. But supervision is not, or should not generally be a kind of Fire Service, dashing from crisis to crisis. Role play will at best rehearse the counsellor in a new perception, a new possibility of insight and response with many more clients than the one who is in the foreground this particular week.

I have remarked that some counsellors who were unfamiliar with role play until they came to supervision with me, have then marched off and set their clients to role play in counselling sessions. The instances that have come back to me have sounded a creative way of letting the client find out or underline something for herself, sometimes at a moment when the counsellor confessed to me that she had to bite back an impulse of her own to advise or moralise.

THE THREE-D DIAGRAM

Another way of allowing a direct experiment, a rehearsal or dry run, in supervision, is to use objects to stand in for people. The most familiar for Gestalt therapists is to let the counsellor speak to an empty chair or cushion, as if they were occupied by the person she is talking about. Then she can change places, and reply to what she has just said, from the other person's stand-point, or rather, sit-point. If you have not tried doing this, you may feel sceptical of what sounds such an awkward and artificial device. As most people who have tried it will tell you, it very often leads quickly to enhanced insight about the effect of each person on the other, and of the subtext, the emotional dialogue that has been going on between them below the words. It is as direct a way as I know to let the supervisee experience the other point of the triangle, the client's.

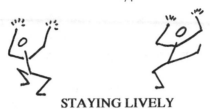

STAYING LIVELY

Creating liveliness in supervision is not merely agreeable; it makes experience vivid, and helps most people to remember clearly what they have learnt. As well as role play, there are many other methods to help you to freshness and attentiveness. In P.N.E.U. schools, I remember, they allege that children's attention span is at best around twenty minutes. So their lessons are constructed in twenty-minute chunks, with deliberate changes of activity or pace. Unless something very absorbing is happening, I doubt that grown-ups reliably have much longer attention, for working in any one particular way.

Responsive dialogue is the central method of supervision I value. Within that, supervisees and supervisors will from time to time need some other experiments to illuminate or reinforce what is being discovered. You may well have invented these or other devices of your own.

TAPES FOR TOTAL RECALL

To my mind tapes are about fifty per cent miracle and fifty per cent curse. The curse is partly just the technology. The damn things do not work consistently well. Sometimes they refuse even to start. The quality on them can be so appalling as to make play-back a penance. Tapes click loudly and run out in the midst of a delicate piece of work, leaving ánxiety about whether to stop everything in order to attend to the machine rather than the person opposite. They are voluminous, and take far more time to riffle through than does a written transcript.

All these are physical objections. Far graver are the ethics of taping. A compliant client may well agree to taping, but really feel thrown off balance by the sense of being recorded. Much more than any other records, tapes are incontrovertible evidence. They are the blackmailers' friend, exposing every word, and on vision-tape every gesture, to whoever picks up the cassette and plays it.

However, from the narrow but important viewpoint of supervision and the counsellor's development, tapes are a most excellent aid. Among much else, they show the supervisor how open the counsellor is to learning about herself, to self-supervision, in other words. Most people are gratifyingly quick to pick up from a witnessed tape play-back their own mannerisms, speech habits, and other subtleties which might be overlooked in another form of supervision.

Trainees need to bring tapes to supervision. As counsellors become more experienced, there is perhaps a more open choice to negotiate between the three parties to supervision, or the four if an agency is involved. Many wise counsellors have the permission of some suitable clients to allow taping from time to time, for the purposes of supervision.

Some supervisees tape their supervision meetings, to play over on long car journeys or at some moment when they are ready to remind themselves of what they and the supervisor said. This seems to me a salutary discipline to the supervisor, to speak clearly and to say only what she feels easy to have played back. I ask counsellors to file any such tapes under lock and key, but do not ask them to destroy them as suggested in the next section.

SECURITY

Sometimes I get the counsellor to ask the client to mark the cassette in a way she can recognise. Then in time the tape can be returned to the client, either verifiably wiped, or for her to wipe. I know that there would have been opportunity for copying the tape in the meantime. But this somewhat laborious procedure usually makes the point that it is meant to: that the counsellor and the invisible supervisor are concerned about the client's privacy.

EDITING

Given that by one means or another a counsellor arrives at supervision with a tape to deal with, you are faced with perhaps fifty minutes of material. I ask the supervisee to edit the tape heavily before she arrives, and if possible bring her own play-back machine, so that the inconsistencies on the counter of my machine and hers do not waste our time. In the editing, she is to limit herself to an agreed amount of play-back, usually adding up in total to no more than about twelve minutes. The rest of the time is for her and my comment. In practice it is rare even to play all the marked sections, since so much reflection is generated by a very little material of this vivid kind.

Sometimes we may be reviewing a session simply to see in a general way how the counsellor is working. In this case, I probably ask her to mark two or three interchanges where she feels pleased with herself for what she achieved. As well, she will point up some places where she is less sure of what she has done.

As you may have observed, most counsellors seem more eager to point out their possible shortcomings, than to underline their successes. So this discipline is designed to improve their perspective on their work. It may with luck remind them too to allow their clients to discuss more than problems and difficulties, and to notice the ways in which they are coping successfully.

When people bring me pre-edited tapes, they make notes beforehand as well. Sometimes they send these in before the session, and I have had a look or listen by the time they arrive. Unless I am paid to do it, I should not like to listen to complete tapes, with all the pauses, inaudible lumps and other grey areas that may well be recorded. It is not in any case usually my job to make a complete evaluation of a session. The counsellor much more usefully does that for herself, and then checks her findings with me or you later on.

PERFORMER IN CONTROL

Sometimes you can get a good impression of your supervisee's work by letting her play back an unedited part of a session, with her finger on the pause button. Again, this is a method that is used very extensively in some training. I like it sometimes. She stops the tape whenever she sees or hears something she wants to comment. You can run the tape back to retrieve moments you want to talk about, if she has omitted them. This method shows not only what goes on in the session, but again gives a glimpse of the internal supervisor in your supervisee, as she critiques what she has done.

MUSCLES AS WELL AS MIND. MORE IDEAS.

THE COMPOSITE COUNSELLOR

Doubling means standing behind someone with your hands on her shoulders, for as long as it takes to utter what you want her to say. An illustration of it was given in the last chapter. If you have not tried doing this, you wonder about the point of it. The best way to find out is just to experiment.

What I like is the economy of this way of working. Rather than have another member of the supervision group go through some lengthy and possibly offensive preamble, such as,

"Well if I was you I'd want to say..." or, *"Why haven't you told him...?"*, the supervisee simply hears the content of an alternative intervention.

In group supervision I use this method very often. It is a way of simulating the discipline of a counselling session, in which the words uttered by the counsellor need to be clear, few and useful. It is tougher to stand and pretend to make an actual counselling intervention, than to loll back in a chair playing the grand old fireside game of *"Haven't you tried?"* It is an exposing and challenging exercise that supervisees learn from quickly.

THE TRIANGLE

From time to time in this book I have brought up the idea of the triangle of Counsellor, Supervisor and, [for the sake of a different initial], Patient. This exercise works directly with this triad. I use it in groups which split into threes, and even with pairs of supervisees, with me as third figure. Each person in the three takes on the role of C, S, or P. The counsellor usually begins in the C position, and responds to questions from the other two. These questions aim to help the supervisee understand more about herself and her client, and move on from whatever difficulty has made her ask for attention.

Here are some of the questions which might occur. The group members have been told the difficulty the counsellor is having. The questions are addressed to her, in whatever role she takes, by the people assuming the other roles at that moment, as:

S: What sort of rapport have you with P?

P: What's your private judgement about how I use these sessions?

When everyone feels ready, the counsellor/supervisee moves to the client position, P, and the others switch roles and question her again.

C: What are you really wanting from me?

S: Tell me what your counsellor is like.

The last shift puts the supervisee in the supervisor position. Perhaps the others suggest

C: Give me your criticisms of what I have been doing.

P: Was my anger last session a transference phenomenon? Or was it mostly to do with my train being cancelled?

I am fond of this exercise. Everyone is engaged in the work. People rise to the subtlety required, and regularly produce questions of great appropriateness. Time and again I suspect that more has been elicited and explored than if I had been the only person responding. All players tend to report insight about their own way of working, gained from intervening in this way on someone else's work.

ATTITUDES

Reasons are the camouflage of the emotions. Much of what is said in a counselling session is likely to be a verbal way of symbolising underlying emotionality, which is attitude.

The client may apparently be talking about her attitudes and responses in the rest of her life. You as an experienced counsellor are aware of how what she says connects too to the present, to what is going on between you and her. All this applies as clearly, in my opinion, to supervision.

To make this more vivid, I like from time to time to invite a supervisee to stop talking, and make a tableau of her and me, or her and anyone else present, which to her mind represents what is going on emotionally in the little system of her-and-the-client.

Once people have grasped this idea, the latent caricaturist or cartoonist in them is likely to emerge to useful effect.

Once you and they have seen this tableau, there is sometimes much to be gained from asking the counsellor to imagine what tableau the other person, the client herself, might set up to portray what is going on between them. It may be a dramatically different picture.

I like too to explore the attitudes between me and the supervisee, with the same device. It can be a way of nipping a collusion in the bud, or revealing some antagonism we have not noticed or admitted. The method is vivid, economical of time, and lets in some of what might be screened out of words. After all, as a species we had an enormous number of generations with vestigial speech, before we became the over-fluent word-bandiers we can be now. We have the equipment to recognise and infer our attitudes to each other without re-symbolising them into speech.

Experiment, if this idea is new to you. The feeling is of using a different part of the mind in doing so. Tableaux reach the parts only words cannot reach.

USING PROPS

Another device which supplements or replaces some words in supervision, has a small overlap with play therapy. Specially in one to one sessions, I sometimes suggest that the supervisee uses some of the shells and pebbles in a bowl on the table near us, to show her version of some scene she is describing.

Denise came to me one day with an involved story of the various agencies a new client was in touch with. I began to be lost in the complexity of the story, and said so. Denise said the same had happened to her when she was with Anne, her client.

She fetched a pile of books from the shelf, and began to build what looked like a version of Stonehenge on the floor. In the middle she put a paeony to represent Anne. I asked what all this was about, not sceptically, but with considerable interest. Denise was concentrating hard, and I trusted that she was finding things out for herself.

"Yes," she said with conviction, looking at the scene. "This is how Anne's world sounds to me. A series of little shelters that she dashes in and out of." I asked where Denise was in the scene. Interestingly, she had forgotten herself. Anne was so busy and earnest that Denise had somehow let herself be tuned out, except as a worried observer. So the sculpt was useful in more than one way. It gave Denise more sense of how her client's world seemed to be set up; and it revealed the oddly guilty and inadequate role she had taken on in relation to Anne. She said it was as if the central statement coming from Anne was that her troubles were so unusual and important that everyone was likely to make a very poor job of sorting them out.

Now I asked Denise to use the books or whatever else she needed from round the room, to set up a picture of how she would like to have her counselling with Anne develop. After a moment, she put the books into two parallel lines.

"*Too many bolt-holes,*" she said darkly. "*Anne goes from the F.S.U. to Social Services to the Tavistock to this charity thing to Samaritans to the community counselling service to a private therapist to the doctor. No! Next time I see her I shall show her my*

picture of all this. And I'll give her the choice. See me OR keep
running around. Not both."

THE TRIANGLE PERCEIVED

People learn best when the learning model presented to them
resembles, or easily adapts to, those they set up in their own minds. I keep
talking about the Triangle. To some people it is on the flat, a plan, perhaps
with equal sides. To others it will immediately translate in their minds to an
elevation, with the supervisor literally in an overview position. Getting
supervisees to imagine and describe or even draw their perceptions of this
triangle, is a greater aid to communication than it might seem.

I remember one supervisee who placed the supervisor almost beside
her, and found this an encouraging configuration. Another had me in the
same place, but with images of a parent breathing down her neck and
cramping her style. Until she had put the supervisor where she wanted to in
a drawing, she did not free herself to be in a useful dialogue in reality.

In the same way, let people take a moment to visualise, to make an
image of, the parallel process, the overlap or lack of overlap they see
between their perceived position with the supervisor, and with the patient.

The supervisor too can learn a great deal for herself from noticing
how she is seeing, and how using, the triangle.

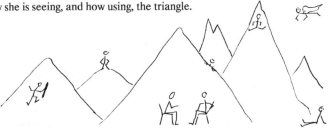

Different supervisees on different days will need different emphases.
Overall, I hope you will agree, much of our work as supervisors is to
encourage them to move flexibly in imagination between all those points.
The better we are at doing that ourselves, the clearer the learning we offer.

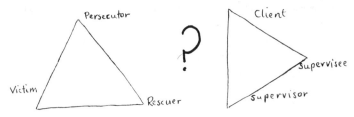

THE ECHO

Time and again, what goes on when a counsellor talks to the supervisor about a client, echoes part of what is going on between the client and counsellor, in their sessions together. The manner of the supervision can for a time be a mirror of the counselling. Parallel process is the slightly mystifying jargon to describe this. As I have noted already, supervisors sometimes concentrate on noticing it, or claiming to notice it, rather in the way that a bird-watcher will suddenly shout

"*A kite! I saw a red kite!*" The event is noted, but no more is done about it. Watching supervisors in training, I have sometimes wished they would jettison this most illuminating concept, if all they can do it about it is bird-spot, and in doing so lose track of the learning opportunity it is.

So let us start simply, with a reminder about what transference is. Like all truth, it can be defined in simple language. It is no more than people's transferring of their expectations in one scene in their life, onto a different scene.

The fun often starts when the people in the second scene get dragged into these expectations, and even begin playing out some version of the drama role which the dominant person has probably unknowingly assigned them.

It looks as if there is a transferential element, an element of projection, in most human interaction. If I am convinced, for example, that Men Are Bullies, then this transference, presumably from the early part of life, is not likely to make me much of a social asset. I am likely to cringe from or avoid men, or perhaps get my bullying in first, and generally be the sort of character people cross off their invitation list.

In fact my father was a wise, lively and generous man. Looking back, I can see how I have transferred this expectation onto other men, who have often brought out that side of themselves with me, to the advantage of both of us. There are disadvantages, too, in social and professional settings, in casting people into roles rather than being open to more of what they perhaps want to express.

In supervision, the transference, parallel process or echo, call it what you will, can be magnificently informative, whoever it stems from. With the details of clients disguised, here are some examples of what I am talking about.

In one group I supervise, people have established a convention of spending the first few minutes of the meeting saying anything they need to get off their chests. Then they state how much time they each need, tailor their needs to reality, and, as they each begin, appoint their own monitor to remind them when their time ration is ending. Today Mary looked hot and bothered, and was unusually strident.

"It's no good," she said , with some defiance, *"I'm absolutely desperate about G., and I've just got to have half an hour at least."*
Someone asked if she had brought a tape of a session.

"G. won't let me tape him." She pouted.

John reminded her that he had agreed at the last meeting to bring a tape and notes about one of his clients to this one. He had been up till very late writing background notes which he had photocopied to circulate to everyone, and he was expecting to take at least an hour.

"Well in the end it doesn't matter if that waits till next week,"
said Mary, whining, but seeming like someone who was certainly going to get her way. *"I tell you, I just feel as if I shall explode if I don't get some help."* As Mary had never been so insistent in the group before, people agreed to give her half an hour. She took some minutes growling and whining more about G., who had obviously made her feel very frustrated. Then she described him, somewhat repetitively, and mostly in terms of his feelings. People had to ask her his age and other measurables, his circumstances, and his presenting difficulties and hopes. In that group the members were used to working from McHugh's (1986) perspectives:

What the client is, (the measurables)

What the client has (symptoms, circumstances)

What the client does (behaviour in and out of the counselling room)

What the client tells (the story by which she makes her own sense of her life).

So it was odd that she did not start her presentation with a thumb-nail sketch along these lines, as members generally did.

"I know he needs help," she kept saying, *"but there just doesn't seem to be any way of getting through to him."*

"You sound as if you're trying too hard," said John. *"Why don't you just stay quiet and let him run out of steam?"*

"I've tried that, and he just talks and talks until I'm lost in what he's saying."

"He's frightened," said Paddy. *"I bet he's too terrified to let you in. What sort of rapport have you tried to make with him?"*

"How on earth can anyone establish rapport with Niagara Falls in the rainy season? That's what he's like."

Watching and feeling, trying to make sense of what was happening in the room, I saw how almost everyone responded to Mary's air of irritated desperation by producing, at considerable speed, Why-Don't-You? suggestions. It was as if they were feeding her good practice-serves in a metaphorical tennis game. This was far from the way they usually worked. What is more, she slammed every suggestion into the net. At last, nettled, someone said,

"I understand how difficult YOU'RE being. You've had forty-five minutes, and all that has happened is that we're all frustrated now."

I suggested that we spend even longer, to work out what was going on. For a start, Mary had not appointed a time monitor, and nobody had pointed that out to her until this minute. In their turn, the rest of the group had seemed to enter into the spirit of things by suggesting, by giving advice, by interrupting, by making what looked like repeated attempts at cosy friendly control. Yet they were people who knew well that Mary had all the resources to work out her own solutions.

They reflected on what had gone on, and I encouraged them to report images of the dialogue. The tennis game was one. Elsie said they had seemed like a lot of dithery maiden aunts trying to be helpful to a great bully of a nephew.

"O," said Mary, *"G. was brought up by two maiden aunts. And he's fattish. I could imagine him being a bully."*

"He bullies you."

She accepted this. The feel of the meeting had changed. We were once again a working group, a co-operative. People took note that they could be magicked, black-magicked even, into a dialogue which everyone knew was useless, and which was a close re-enactment of the frustrating sessions with G. More than that, from Elsie's highly intuitive image about the dithery aunts, we were able to guess that the sort of exchange we had plunged into was one G. had been engaged in since early in his life. So we were contemplating two-stage magic. G. somehow converted Mary into his dithery aunt, or, more accurately, she took on that role with him. Then, hey presto, she played G. and we played the aunts when she came to talk about him.

You notice that I asked group members for their images, rather than for their rational responses about the scene we had acted out. This calling up of associations, of uncensored pictures, is often a high road to new awareness.

Time and again, a simile, a fantasy, is a vivid clue to a temporarily bemused supervisee. An image may bring a sudden clarity about the ways in which the counsellor, or a whole group has perhaps been over-influenced by the moods and preoccupations of a dominant client.

So, as well as everything else it can be, supervision can be likened to a hill, where echoes of a counselling session, and echoes of the client's way of getting on with people, can clearly be heard if you listen out for them. The hill is not the counselling session. It is a place from which you can look back at it with a wider perspective.

The high art of supervising is in part to do with keeping an eye on the range of hills or triangles round the counsellor, and encouraging her to move around them easily and informedly. Then she will be able to see the landscape of her client's life, her own, the counselling, and the supervisory relationship, from different points of view. The next section expands this idea.

THE GEOMETRY OF COUNSELLING

Part of the job of supervising is to stay aware of the three points of a triangle, and make sure that the counsellor switches between them appropriately herself. There is the client's point of view, which may take in both his habitual attitudes, and whatever is likely to be going on for him in response to what the counsellor has or has not done there and then. There is the counsellor's point of view, in terms of her feelings, understanding and skills. And there is the supervisor's point of view, as this person who is outside the two-person system, looking down from the top of the hill. The counsellor needs to be able to move to this position too. Patrick Casement (1985) refers to the Internal Supervisor who needs to be there throughout sessions. Richard Bandler (1975) talks of the Dissociated position, with much of the same meaning.

In this extract, notice the switches from viewpoint to viewpoint.

JANEY: *Um. Anyway, where was I? O yes. Um. This client of mine seems, er...*

S: *What's going on? I'm ready to fall asleep!*

JANEY: *Sorry. I was a bit preoccupied.*

S: (elicits counsellor phenomenology) *See if you recall what was preoccupying you.*

JANEY: (guesses at client's view) *Different possibilities of what might really be going wrong for this client.*

S: (supervisor phenomenology) *Let's look a bit more at what was going on for me just then, to see if it gives us any clues. I was starting to get indignant over here, as well as tired. I felt extinguished, put aside. I had the fantasy you didn't notice I was here.*

JANEY: *That's just how he makes me feel.*

S: *Now I'm moving from just the emotionality, to playing with the idea that we've partly shuffled into each other's roles. You're playing him, and I'm playing you, emotionally. Tell some more about that preoccupation you mentioned.*

JANEY: *I felt doom-laden to the point of being, well, in a frozen panic.* [She paused] *Yes, maybe that is what I need to register. He is so stuck in terror and denying terror, that he will have very little attention free for noticing me.*

S*: Tell me what you are saying about yourself, in saying that.*

JANEY: [Laughs ruefully] *O lumme, here I go again. Janey doesn't count.*

S: *You see this client. I don't see him. So your judgement is very likely indeed to be better than mine about what you do when you are with him. But I want you to give me your impression at this moment of how stuck he really is, and how much he can cope with noticing you. In T.A. language, how much adult is available in him?*

JANEY*: Well of course, he does have rather a high-flying job.*

S: *I was thinking of that. Yet anyone eavesdropping on us these last few minutes might get the impression he was about ready for custodial care! So you know that he can cope with the world very well in some ways. Are you still stuck in the echo effect with him, in an echo of how he influences many people to respond to him?*

JANEY: *Hm. I really had started thinking of him as such a poor frail chap! I had better put up with being mesmerised to unconsciousness, or he would feel upset. I've learned something.*

Even if we had not been in what I call the echo, I think I would have been doing a better job in saying that I had got bored or sleepy or numb, than in pretending. If I spend my time as a supervisor trying to preserve a false image of myself, then it is possible that my behaviour will echo back into the counselling, as the counsellor copies me and does the same to her client.

As the vast bulk of what brings people to seek counselling is to do with their difficulties in getting on with others, the least we professionals can do is offer our own straightforwardness. They may not be in touch with their own.

You may have noticed that, though I began this chapter on the echo of the counselling session that often comes into the supervision room, other echoes are around too. I have just spoken of the echo that can, and I know often does, go back from supervision to the counselling. Then too, in the extract of the supervision with Mary, we came on the perhaps more obvious sort of echo: the client in the session echoes other scenes in his life.

In the picture, then, I put hills or triangles for the supervisor to keep in her awareness and bring to the attention of the supervisee. First there is the three-person pattern of client, counsellor and supervisor. Then there is the triangle of transference. This is the client's movement between

The I-Thou of the immediate session in the room;

The general present of her preoccupations about work, partner and other day-to-day topics;

The third angle is her early life and its shaping of her present attitude and responses.

At times the supervisor will do well to bring the counsellor's own triangle of transference into the conversation - and her own.

Here is the familiar Drama Triangle of Victim, Persecutor and Rescuer. As you may remember, once into this configuration, it often proves much easier to jump or slither between the different roles, than to bust the game by refusing to play. It is very important for you as a supervisor to notice if you are lapsing into a point on this hideous triangle.

Do you suddenly feel defensive of the absent client, and consequently blaming of the counsellor? Do you suddenly notice that you are mounting an unnecessary rescue, by offering handy hints from your own counselling repertoire? The counsellor would probably learn far more by facing that she is floundering with her client, and then devising her own way through her difficulty.

As a counsellor or as a supervisor, part of your work is to talk about what is going on unsaid between you and the person opposite. If you keep quiet about this emotional process, whether it is a change of pace or manner in the other, or your own responses to her and what she is saying and how you feel treated, then you lose effectiveness. You will do respectable, mechanical work, maybe. But you will leave out huge areas of potential learning for the person with you. And you will leave out risk and excitement and learning for yourself.

To finish this subject here, I want to remind you of an important simplicity. Direct statements that start with I can be incontrovertible. They are about your experience, on which you are the world's only authority. Statements that start with you are often guesses. I come across people who remember this when they are counselling. Then as supervisors they go down, or bounce up, with acute bouts of the dread but often undiagnosed disease, Omnipotent Thinking, whose symptoms may include Second Sight and Alleged Infallible Accurate Empathy.

In the chapter on style there is more about which part of the system of supervisor-and-counsellor, or counsellor-and-client, you comment. Whether or not you are self-disclosing, I suggest that the point of reference you need to acknowledge inside yourself, is what is happening to you in the moment. You may be playing echo to your counsellor's client's Grandad. You may be dragging the effects of last night's party into the session. You may be in a moment of clear recognition and synergy. If you fail to make a comment and enquiry, you will never know.

THE ANNUAL REVIEW

Many counsellors build into their work an occasional review session, when with their client they look back at what they have done or not done, and forward to what they might tackle next. These people are likely to understand the usefulness in supervision too, of this deliberate stepping back to take a critical look. This section is about ways of setting up and using such a review, as supervisor and supervisee.

The first step is to moot the idea, and set a time for discussing it. If you rush straight into the discussion, the counsellor is at a disadvantage: you have already been brooding about the subject; that is why you raised it. She has probably thought about it a good deal less. She may need to know, specially if she is a student, whether she is scared of the idea, against it, or in danger of just going along uncritically with your plans, without her own investment.

When you do discuss it, what needs to be decided is

When

What for

How

It might be easy to think that the *What For* is implicit in the task of review. Rather than jog along on that assumption, make space for you both to talk about what you might get out of doing it. Is the review all to be about the counsellor? Is there to be mutuality, with talk too about how you are doing as supervisor? Are you going to give space to thinking about specific further training? Will you make an opportunity for changing how supervision happens in future? You may be a wonderful supervisor; but in terms of career development, would your supervisee do well to think about trying a different person, perhaps from a different discipline, or the opposite sex?

The *What For* gives proper importance to the context of the counsellor's work. This may on some occasions usefully extend to looking at how far her practice is in line with her philosophy. Another time, it might be about how she is living her life at the moment, and whether counselling is still the proper work for her. If she is in therapy, she may not need to do this. But many counsellors have no other professional to talk to than you. The *What For* may therefore once in a while take in thinking about a career change or development.

At best, the review can be a very exciting occasion, for taking a large view, and making new plans. For each review to be effective, the counsellor as well as you as supervisor need to know your answers to the *What For*.

The *How* can also be expressed in some reminder questions, including

Who is going to write something?

What is she going to write?

What is going to be done with the writing?

Years of being school-children have lodged in us the model of teacher writing a report, which we wait, probably trembling, to see torn from its envelope by a parental figure. If anything about this way of starting the review appeals to you, then a variant is to ask the pupil to write a similar report about teacher. In other words, if you write about your supervisee, she writes about you. Then if you wish you can both go through the envelope-opening experience, and read the reports through before you meet to talk through what has been said.

This appeals to me a good deal less than its opposite, which is to have the supervisee write a report on herself, which she submits to you, either beforehand, or when you meet to discuss the contents. As you will not need to be reminded if you have done such a thing, writing a report on yourself, which is to be talked over with another, albeit friendly, person, is a great deal more challenging than sitting around and simply uttering a few items of appropriate self-criticism, which can easily be chucked back into the trash-cans of your mind if they feel uncomfortable.

From this you gather that I am in favour of doing some writing, rather than having just a verbal exchange. Selective amnesia is the enemy of such talk. On many occasions I have observed how people manage to jettison into some unlit corner of their minds, the shrewd, kindly, well-worded and useful descriptions of them that are made by themselves and others in conversation.

On a counselling course where I lectured, we used the device of having each of a group of ten people take turns once a year to sit in the hot seat, and hear back one sentence that each other person present needed to say to them.

Most students promptly forgot whatever praise or appreciation was voiced, and held on to any piece of carping, whether it seemed very relevant or not. A few did the opposite, and managed not to hear overt or implicit complaint or criticism. The one rescuing statement put in by some tender-hearted or hypocritical peer would be all they chose to keep available to awareness.

The exercise became far more effective when we asked the person on the hot seat to appoint a scribe, who wrote down the statements for her. If she wrote for herself, that too seemed to take away from the occasion, by keeping her out of contact with the speakers. Later she made a fair copy for herself of these notes, and at the next meeting was asked to make some comment on them, in the same group. In this way we incorporated a form of Telling Back, which is a most effective reinforcer of learning, into the exercise.

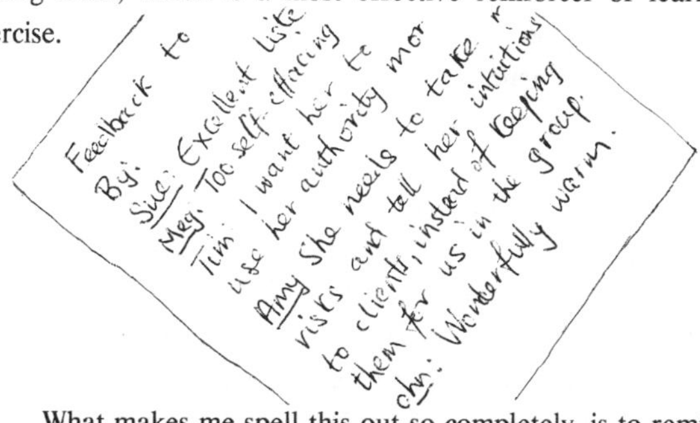

[handwritten note]

What makes me spell this out so completely, is to remind you of the possibility of using a form of the same exercise as a supervision review, if you are dealing with one person or a group who are reluctant to sit at home by themselves to do their writing.

If you are in a group, take care to remind the person in the hot seat that she too is a member of the group, and needs to add her own comment about herself to those of the others. Unless this happens, you are back with a spoken version of the school report.

If the person being judged adds her own judgement, she has the opportunity to think in a properly critical, rather than just a defensive way, about herself. One of two outcomes is likely. Either she will say something of value to herself; or she will be inappropriately defensive. In the latter case, if she is in a group of counsellors who are competent enough to be practising at all, she will be sussed. The occasion may become a little nerve-wracking; it will also be an excellent reminder to everyone present of how to deal with someone who is being avoidant. It will be an implicit piece of training for counselling, as well as an important task in its own right.

As may have occurred to you already, many of the devices I suggest here for a supervision review, may be adapted by the counsellor for any review sessions she has with a client. In the same way, you may have methods of reviewing with your counselling clients, that will work too with supervisees.

In individual supervision there are still ways of making some of whatever writing there is to be, take place at and after the review session, rather than before it. Both people may want to make a few notes before their meeting. Then together they talk their way through their formal or informal agenda, of which I shall speak later. Once again, it may be valuable to have each make notes for the other person, rather than herself.

Then in private, both write up an expanded version of these notes, to present and discuss next time they meet, with a view to altering them if necessary, to produce a document that both people agree. This part is important. There is sometimes an amazing difference between what I think someone has taken as the spirit and letter of a discussion, and what they put on paper about it afterwards. Though I tell supervisees not to expect their clients to understand them all the time, I can still be surprised that communication can falter just as much in supervision.

In training, most people who go in for this profession respond gratefully to the injunction to be open to self and open to others. That ethos stays with most supervisees. Then here and there I find good practitioners who grow a little defensive, over used to their own well-tried methods and assumptions. The review is a way of licensing a bit of healthy boat-rocking.

These wry remarks apply with just as much force to supervisors, who may get particularly used to hearing themselves hold forth to younger people, who possibly give them even a shade more reverence than they inevitably deserve. Hence my enthusiasm for making the review a two-way affair.

WHAT TO TALK ABOUT

The widest trawl is perhaps the impressionistic exercise I spoke of earlier in this chapter. In a group of more than a very few people, there is a good chance of achieving a useful picture of any member by no more than inviting people to say what they need to say to her, in the context of her as a counsellor.

The opposite end of the spectrum is to procure one of the many performance scales popular in management circles, adapt it to counselling, and let the supervisee mark herself and or you on ratings of one to ten on a series of abstractions, such as clarity, attentiveness, concern, or whatnot.

To my mind this is a somewhat airy-fairy exercise, even though it leads to rows of figures that look splendidly measured and irrefutable. If the supervisee is prepared to ask some of her clients to fill in the scales too, she may arrive at a more useful read-out. What is most important is to use such an exercise as the basis of a discussion which leads to action. Some of the needed questions here are:

What are you and she going to do less of and more of?

How will you set that up?

How will you monitor yourselves?

This is as good a place as any to state my belief that any review which does not have a recognisable and monitored effect on future behaviour, might as well not take place. A review is not about the bolstering of complacency, nor yet about the tidy apportioning of blame. It is about a co-operative look at what has been, is, and can enjoyably and usefully be in the future.

As I mentioned earlier in this chapter, a creative way in to the review is to consult your supervisee about what she sees as the most valuable method, and the most valuable focus, for her.

As part of the exercise, she may for example decide to take one of her counselling sessions, and go through it in detail, rating herself on some such system as John Heron's *Six Categories of Intervention.* Doing this produces more than an appearance of hard data. It will show her and you just how much she interrogates, confronts, and so on. It can be a sound basis for planning next year's development. Or she may ask you to view one of her sessions through two-way mirror or on tape. In other words, she is quite likely to come up with ideas that you have not thought of, and from which you both benefit.

Whatever the form of the review, I imagine it working well if in some way it lets the following questions be answered.

What do I want more of, less of and maintained?

What do I want the same, more of, less of from you?

What have I achieved?

What have I not done that I wanted to?

What are the stoppers?

What do I want to do next?

What needs to happen so that I can?

What do I need from you to help me?

How shall we know when we've got there?

How shall we monitor as we go?

When?

These questions are intended for the counsellor's review of her work. So, as well as some mutuality, as I have already stressed, I see it as proper that most of the attention is on the counsellor's work, and on her relation with the supervisor. If the supervisor, as I hope she will, wants an exhaustive review for herself, I doubt if she should try to get it in the time the counsellor is paying to have with her. I hope that comment shows how I see the bulk of the time of the review being focussed.

The first question gives space for a wide look at how the counsellor sees herself doing her job. The next lets her give her view of the supervisor. The later ones only apply if the counsellor wants to make some alteration in her way of working. If she does not, then I am a bit alarmed. Innate scepticism keeps me from supposing that you are supervising the Perfect Counsellor.

The last three questions are designed to give reality to what at the time of the review can only be ideas. I remember one counsellor who at her review told me that she had time and money for some more training, but was not clear in just what area. We worked out a kind of shopping period, of the summer months, when she would go on various short courses. Then we set a date in our diaries for talking over where she was getting to.

I emphasise the usefulness of taking out your diaries at a review session, and marking a date or dates when you will look at progress on the counsellor's change of intervention strategy, her shift to a specialised area, or whatever else you have talked over, and are in danger of letting slide unless you build in the steps to encouragement and success.

An aspect of behavioural counselling that I respect is the co-operative goal-setting, the close and realistic monitoring, and the emphasis that if the client falls down on achieving her goal, the counsellor has some responsibility in that. She was part of the goal-setting, and may have colluded with an unrealistic ambition. In just the same way, the supervisor's task in a review is perhaps to temper the ambitions of the counsellor to what is attainable in terms of time and that counsellor's character.

In a specially vivid way the review points up the supervisor's central task. She is there to encourage and assist the supervisee to become the best counsellor she can possibly be for her clients. That best will in part be to do with psychological theory, and with the detailed examination of how and what she communicates to her client. The best is also to do with living in a way that leaves the counsellor free to love. The review is a chance to look at whether supervision, which mostly means you as supervisor, is taking the supervisee forward at the right pace towards self-confidence based on reality, towards valuing of herself and others, towards, in short, what Maslow (1962) called *Abundance Motivation*.

LOOKING AFTER YOURSELF

Recent codes of practice for supervisors require them to have the supportive monitoring that I advocated in the first edition of this book. It sounds right, in a profession dedicated to mental or psychic health, to enable that in counsellor and supervisor, so that they are free to promote it for the client.

In training institutions, staff who work as supervisors already have a good deal of contact with each other. Supervisors who work alone may seem quite isolated. All of them need occasional focussed meetings, in pairs or other configurations which allow them some overview of their own work, and the way other people in the same position are dealing with the same kinds of issues and difficulties that they encounter.

DEFINING SUPERVISION, CONSULTANCY AND MENTORING

This seems as good a place as any to say a little about the differences between these activities. For our purposes, supervision is for the most part directly to do with clinical issues. As has been stated in several places in this book, it exists for the benefit of the client.

Consultancy in this context is a more eclectic activity. It takes in much that is to do with the supervisor's, and often an organisation's, good. Some of it will be at strategic and tactical level, about non-counselling interventions, such as induction seminars, training for managers or staff in counselling skills, and so forth. The consultant's task is to help problem-solve. Perhaps you know the following wry definition of a consultant, as someone who borrows your watch from you to tell you what time it is.

This is not altogether disreputable, if you would not look at the watch yourself. I am repeatedly struck by the way in which people who come to supervision or for consultancy present all the material necessary for an aha! experience, for a breakthrough of awareness. But they have not configured all this data; it is like a jumble of jigsaw pieces, all present but not assembled. The consultant is in a sense being handed the watch to read. In another vocabulary, it looks as if talking to someone is needed for the completion of that gestalt, or, two heads are better than one.

Mentoring is more like supervision, except that it is not about clinical practice. It is a co-operative look by mentor and a particular person in an organisation at what he or she is currently doing. Like supervision, its aim is to help raise awareness and increase their choice about what they are about. Like supervision, it is a supportive and encouraging activity, with the interests of an invisible third party, in this case the organisation, well in the foreground. In my view mentoring does not exist solely and primarily for the benefit of the organisation, however. It is also a chance for the person being mentored to evaluate whether he is in the right place, or should change jobs or make some larger career move.

Sometimes I come across consultancy and mentoring which has a smack of the conspiratorial, of Us-Against-The-Authorities, about it. Once in a very long while such a stance is justified, where there is a dubious organisation. Most of the time, no-one is well served by this form of subversion.

The meetings which supervisors have, to look after themselves, are likely to be mostly a species of mentoring.

Even though the supervisors in the arrangement may apparently be freelance, they are ever more likely to be attached to an accrediting body, which is their umbrella organisation. Their relationship to that is important. Unless they communicate within that organisation, and feed it in some measure with more than their annual registration fee, they are avoiding responsibility. It is very easy to slip into criticism of organisational decrees and decisions, without taking part in those decisions, and without making informed and dialogic representations in the right places to get them altered.

Some years ago I came across the strange case of Mrs Cribbens and her carpenter. In a negative, but I think quite funny way, it illustrates the need for distinction between supervision, mentoring and consultancy.

THE STRANGE CASE OF MRS CRIBBENS

Mrs Cribbens turned up at a social work agency of a specialist kind. She was a very dithery lady by all reports, apparently hell-bent on creating debt, chaos and discomfort for all around her.

The agency was funded to deal with people of a certain disability, with which Mrs Cribbens had indeed some slight, even tenuous connection. However, they were very short of clients. They took on Mrs Cribbens, who stated as her presenting problem that she needed a carpenter, as two in succession had walked out, leaving her kitchen unusable to the point of having no floorboards.

After a case-conference about her, a counsellor attempted to lead Mrs Cribbens into listening to herself, getting in touch with her underlying denied emotionality and so forth.

Mrs Cribbens kept on about the carpenter.

In a dizzy moment the counsellor gave her the name of a good one. The next week Mrs Cribbens had turned her attention to electricians.

At this point the counsellor's supervisor, another member of the agency, pointed out the foolishness of offering this sort of information. The two of them evaluated what distress patterns in the counsellor had led her into this error, and they devised new strategies for bringing Mrs Cribbens to awareness of the possibility of considering a whole new way of life.

The supervisor then talked to her principal about what she had done. Parallel processes of dither proliferated. As they at that point had no other clients at all, the principal got in touch with the regional director, and the two of them made a long shrewd evaluation of what the counsellor and Mrs Cribbens should be doing.

A meeting was set up with the supervisor to pass on their thoughts, which passed in Chinese Whispers back to the counsellor. When an outside consultant, arrived on the scene she was told extremely little about the organisation, and a lot about Mrs Cribbens.

All the people involved were apparently looking to justify their salaries by how well they could do by Mrs Cribbens. They might have done better to allow for the element of projection, and look inwards and contemplate a whole new way of life, in the way they were so keen that Mrs Cribbens should do.

The consultant suggested appropriate publicity for the service, which soon had enough genuine clients to keep their counsellors occupied. Mrs Cribbens found an electrician and left.

One of the lessons in this story is about bad supervising. The supervisor here apparently helped invent a strategy for help that Mrs Cribbens had never sought. She wanted a Yellow Pages Service. She probably thought that she was going to a kind of Citizens' Advice Bureau, which turned out to take a puzzling interest in her soul.

The supervisor did what I would call piggy-back counselling, metaphorically hoisting herself onto the counsellor's back and talking over her shoulder at the client, without ever having clapped eyes on that poor person. The client is always educating, or trying to educate the counsellor, about what she needs. Mrs Cribbens was wonderfully direct. She wanted a carpenter and an electrician, and when she had them, she went away.

After that two more layers of the hierarchy went in for the same activity, vicarious counselling. Everyone in the organisation had experience of counselling, and enjoyed this craft skill rather more than the administrative duties then new to them. No-one was managing the organisation, in a proactive way. No-one was mentoring, helping another colleague to evaluate their role and performance in general in this crisis context.

Calling in the outside consultant was wise, in that that person stuck to her brief, and offered consultancy about increasing the effectiveness of the organisation, as she had been asked to do. An emotional plague was rife, and it probably needed an outsider at that moment to reduce the feverishness around.

THE REFERENCE GROUP

People tend to work best when they have a reference group of others in roughly the same line, whom they respect and can at least occasionally talk to face to face. Role models has become the fashionable term to describe part of this function. Companionship and mutual mentoring and consultancy are other aspects. They need a colleague group or network through which they can encourage and monitor themselves as they go through their careers.

In saying this I need to make clear that I am not at all in favour of supervisory activities as a huge part of life. They keep their value best if not over-indulged.

But now that there is a demand for continuing training as well as some form of mentoring for supervisors, it is worth devising forms to make that easier to achieve.

One is a group which meets three or four weekends a year, sometimes with an invited trainer or consultant, sometimes with the task of peer supervision or mentoring or even training, if members have specialist skills to pass on. If the group is large, it can stand the price of visiting staff better. And the disadvantages are likely to include an informal sub-grouping into smaller bands of buddies, who may be seen as cliques by other members. A smaller group is probably nearer the size of therapeutic group any of the members work in in other settings. Some of the analogies of the dynamics in these different settings may be of value to members. But if one or two members are away for any reason, the group may feel small and forlorn. The following chapter is about configurations for supervision. The Network idea in some modified form might work well for a Supervisors' Group.

Conferences and seminars for supervisors are becoming more common, and at the moment of writing, tend to include demonstrations of supervision. These are potentially of great use to supervisors, but to my mind are not a substitute for some kind of continuing network or group. This latter provides the informed colleague to be in touch with in an emergency. It may furnish a couple of friends who will undertake to clear up your practice if you are suddenly removed from the scene. And if it is composed well, it gives you the sense of having allies behind you in times of trouble or challenge.

A CRITICAL LIST OF CONFIGURATIONS

Let yourself think over the kind of supervision you want to give or receive, at your stage of your working life. A third-year student is likely to have different needs from a therapist of many years' practice. Someone seeing a few people in a voluntary setting may have different needs again from a full-time professional.

Your own professional body will have rules or guide-lines on how much supervision is expected. You need to feel secure, too, about the frequency of supervision. Every term-time week is what many students accustom themselves to.

Thereafter, supervision is required by some bodies in the ratio of one hour to every sixteen or so hours with clients. In later life, if you work for an agency that allows you supervision, the budget may well affect the number of times you meet. The same may apply if you pay for yourself. The practices you have agreed to in your professional body must not be forgotten, though. Paid supervision can usefully be alternated with a peer pair or group. But more of that later.

I have a good deal of evidence that uninspired or wrong-headed supervision can be done in any setting. I have hard evidence too that excellent work can be done in many conventional and unconventional configurations, some of which are listed here.

Some good supervisors charge a lot of money. So do some awful ones, to my mind. Some of the best supervision I have ever had was well on in life, in a peer group, for no money. So, if you are free to choose how you are supervised, consider your needs, and creative ways to meet them, rather than looking first at the constraints on you. To help your imagination, here is a reminder list of some configurations.

[1] REGULAR ONE TO ONE SESSIONS with a designated supervisor, probably from your own discipline or training establishment. This is usually the first, and sometimes the only kind of supervision some people have. For anyone in training, this can be of enormous influence, and at best of inspiration too. *"There needs to be supervisory holding by an experienced person who believes in the student's potential to be in tune with the patient and to comment helpfully."* (Casement 1985)

[2] REGULAR ONE TO ONE SESSIONS WITH A SUPERVISOR FROM A DIFFERENT DISCIPLINE. If this comes about because that supervisor is the only one you know of within fifty miles, there may be a sense of compromise in choosing her or him. If the choice is to do with extending your range, both of you need to acknowledge that, and find ways to include some discussion of your different philosophies and methods in your hours together.

[3] ONE TO ONE PEER SUPERVISION, in which each of you alternate roles. You may alternate from week to week, so first one, then the other has a whole session focussing on her work with clients. Or you may alternate within the session, so both have a chance to deal with some of your preoccupations about how you are working.

On postgraduate training courses I have introduced this way of working, alongside sessions with a staff supervisor. In this way, people overtly learn to supervise as well as to counsel.

In all these one to one arrangements, there is much to be said for letting the supervision session reflect the amount of time the supervisee would spend with a patient or client. This allows a training in pacing. Fifty minutes or an hour is thus a likely duration.

[4] GROUP SUPERVISION WITHIN YOUR DISCIPLINE. Some group supervision is mostly individual supervision with a sympathetic audience, on the understanding that one or two named members will present detailed accounts of their work with one patient, on any particular week.

 At the other end of the spectrum, it can be a slightly frantic jostle, where everyone wants their turn, and the supervisor may feel like a bird confronted with five or ten gaping beaks in a crowded and noisy nest.

Again, the supervisor can be used to chair a valuable exchange between informed people, the group members, rather than to represent the Voice of Truth for the group.

The echo comes back from counselling into a group as well as into a pair. Sometimes it is exaggerated, with different members seeming to take on different aspects of the system being discussed. This is true whether an individual or a therapy group is being presented. There is enormous learning in allowing these echoes into awareness, and working from phenomenological dialogue between all the members of the supervisory group.

Again, a corollary of this is that you may need to look out for a supervisor who is used to working at this subtle level, if you want to be supervised in this way,

[5] GROUP SUPERVISION IN A HYBRID GROUP. For this you need a supervisor who is experienced at working with groups. At best she will also be at home with most of the disciplines in the room. If the group members are experienced, however, then knowing all about Moreno and all about Melanie Klein may be less important for the supervisor, than knowing how to enable people to use the group to best effect.

[6] PEER GROUP SUPERVISION. Before you have much experience, you are likely to have well-founded suspicions about your own skills. So you need someone with more experience to help you discover what on earth else you might do with this depressed or that evasive client. A time comes when you have practised your own discipline enough to feel reasonably confident within it.

You may know this is where you have got to, when you begin to feel dissatisfied with the constraints of, say, endless two-chair work, or forever offering careful interpretations. Further training is one answer. Another is to meet people from other disciplines, to let them look with their eyes at your work, and so to enrich your own ways of responding by learning from your peers.

The length of a group supervision session needs to represent a balance between the number of people in the group, the frequency of meeting, and everyone's attention span. If the group is large, then it will be more effective if members work in sub-groups or pairs for part of the time. On one training, the senior students spent the first half-hour of their group supervision time in pairs which aimed to elicit their preoccupations, and deal with those that could be dealt with, leaving the puzzling bits for the whole group later.

Noticing the thematic connections between what is presented by different members often helps shape the session.

[7] NETWORK SUPERVISION. This is a combination of group and pairs. A number of people who want supervision meet as a group at, say, monthly intervals. They may meet with an outside supervisor, or as a peer group. The meeting will consist partly of case presentation, or some other form of direct supervision. It is also the forum for discussing some of what goes on at interim, probably weekly, meetings, of pairs of group members. Partner swapping can be arranged, and difficulties dealt with.

I invented this model, and shall not be surprised to find that many other people have invented it as well, since it is so useful. The first motive for me was to find a way to stay in touch with postgraduates who worked odd hours, lived at a distance from each other, were short of money, and still wanted to work with me.

Our monthly meetings, which lasted three hours, let me do some overview work with them, and let them all meet each other. The pairs between whiles gave scope for everyone to have more individual attention, combined with flexible times and journeys. At the same time, they were all in fact training themselves as supervisors. And we spent some of our monthly meetings working at how they could do that better.

[8] TRIAD SUPERVISION. This is an informed extension of the common training device of working in threes, with one person as counsellor, one as client and one observer. By halfway through training, this observer role can well be extended, and re-named supervisor. For perhaps the only time in the counsellor's career, all three angles of the supervisory triangle are present at one time. The temporary supervisor can practice challenging

the counsellor to account for what she did at different moments. The client will be there to say what was really going on for her. From this book or other sources the person in that role can equip herself to work overtly at supervisory skills, at the same time as the other two work at the skills of being client and counsellor.

This list may serve to jolt you into thinking of yet a different way of working. Good. Whatever the style, you need to be sure that the person being supervised is

Held, listened to, encouraged;
Challenged, confronted, stimulated;
Disciplined, informed, answerable.

REFERENCES

Bacon F. *Religious Meditations.*
Beaumont F. (1608) *The Maid's Tragedy.*
Bernard J. and Goodyear R. (1992) *Fundamentals of Clinical Supervision.* New York: Alyn and Bacon.
Bion W. (1961) *Experiences in Groups.* London: Tavistock.
Buber M. (1970) *I and Thou.* New York: Scriveners.
Casement P. (1985) *On Learning from the Patient.* London: Tavistock.
Feltham C. and Dryden W. (1994) *Developing Counsellor Supervision.* London: Sage.
French M. (1991) *Beyond Power.* London: Cardinal.
Foucault M. (1980) *Power/Knowledge* Ed. Colin Gordon. New York: Pantheon.
Houston G. (1993) *Being and Belonging.* Chichester and New York: John Wiley.
Houston G. (1995) *The Red Book of Gestalt.* (revised ed.) London: Rochester Foundation.
Illich I. (1973) *Tools for Conviviality.* New York: Harper and Row.
Inskipp F. and Proctor B. (1993) *The Art, Craft and Tasks of Counselling Supervision.* London: Cascade.
Klein M. and Riviere J. (1952) *Developments in Psycho-Analysis.* London: Hogarth Press.
Maslow A. (1962) *Towards a Psychology of Being.* Princeton N.J.: van Nostrand.
McHugh P. and Slavney P. (1986) *The Perspectives of Psychiatry.* Baltimore: Johns Hopkins University Press.
Nietzsche F. (1982) *The Will to Power* Trans. Kauffmann W. U.S.: Viking Penguin.
Page S. and Wosket V. (1994) *Supervising the Counsellor - a Cyclical Model* London: Routledge.
Perls F., Hefferline R. and Goodman P. (1951) *Gestalt Therapy: Excitement and Growth in the Human Personality.* New York: Julian Press. Vol 2. Ch 9.
Russell B. Nobel Prize acceptance speech *Human Society in Ethics and Politics.*
Stern D. (1985) *The Interpersonal World of the Infant.* New York: Basic Books.
Wilson E. (1980) *Sociobiology* Harvard University Press.

AUTHOR

Gaie Houston, M.A. Oxon., Dip. App. B. Sc., has worked as a trainer, counsellor, supervisor, group and organisational consultant and mentor since she trained in the States in the late sixties. She was a lecturer on the S. W. London Counselling Course for seven years, and helped to make it student-centred. She is now Emeritus Adviser to the Gestalt Centre, London, with whom she has worked over the last fifteen years, as well as being a visiting lecturer in Sweden, Norway, Denmark and The United States, and supervising individuals and groups in many settings.

Her recent books are:

BEING AND BELONGING (1993) Chichester: John Wiley.

Then come books in her own imprint:

THE RED BOOK OF GESTALT (Enlarged and revised edition. 1995)

THE RED BOOK OF GROUPS

SUPERVISION AND COUNSELLING (Enlarged and revised edition. 1995)

All titles in this paperback *Red Book* series by Gaie Houston are available from bookshops or direct from

8, Rochester Terrace,
London NW1 9JN. U. K.

Cheques for £5.85 a copy should be made out to Gaie Houston and sent with your order to this address.